CU00594909

The Motorist's Guide to the Law

by Jane Benjamin, Solicitor

London
Fourmat Publishing
1993

ISBN 1 85190 189 2

First published 1986
Second edition 1993

A catalogue record for this book is available from the
British Library

Jane Benjamin is the pen name of a solicitor with special
knowledge of road traffic law.

Printed and bound by
Hartnolls Ltd, Bodmin, Cornwall

© 1986, 1993
Published by Fourmat Publishing, 133 Upper Street,
London N1 1QP

Foreword to the first edition

Since you have opened this book, it is not unreasonable to assume that you are a motorist or perhaps planning to become one. But why should you be tempted to read this guide to motoring law?

Whether you have been driving for many years, or are yet to pass your test, the law which regulates how you may behave on the road applies equally. There are over 15 million private vehicles registered in England and Wales. This makes it easier to understand today's bustling road conditions, which in turn almost inevitably increase your chances of being prosecuted for a road traffic offence at some stage in your driving career. Since many offences are committed in ignorance, the object of this book is to make you aware of the pitfalls which you face each time you venture out onto the road. However, you will probably be relieved to learn that it does not dwell upon legal theory, but instead attempts to explain a complicated subject in a practical way.

Within these covers the most common motoring offences are discussed in detail; the penalty points system and the law on drinking and driving are explained. You will find, too, helpful information on how to conduct your own case without the expense of instructing a solicitor, and where all else fails, how to compose that difficult letter in "mitigation" with a view to a lesser fine. Also dealt with is the fixed penalty system.

You may conclude that given the level of fines, penalty points and periods of disqualification the Courts can impose, reading this book now could pay dividends later and enhance your chances of keeping an endorsement-free driving licence.

James Mathers

Foreword to the second edition

In July 1992 a new Road Traffic Act came into force and made substantial changes to the catalogue of offences which it is possible for a motorist to commit. For example, the old and difficult-to-prove offence of reckless driving (difficult because the Court had to be sure of what was going on in the driver's head at the crucial time) has been replaced by a rather more straightforward offence called dangerous driving which focuses on the nature of the driving itself. Furthermore, in response to mounting public concern about the terrible devastation often caused by intoxicated drivers, an entirely new and very serious offence of causing death by careless driving whilst under the influence of drink or drugs has been created. Changes have also been made to the penalty points system, and compulsory retesting is now a certainty for those who drive dangerously and a possibility for those who commit other offences.

As if these changes were not enough to cope with, in October 1992 a new system of imposing fines was introduced into magistrates' courts. It is called the "unit fine" system and it requires the court to assess the penalty for an offence as a number of units on a scale and then multiply that figure by the offender's "disposable weekly income" in order to produce the amount of money he or she actually has to pay. The object of that exercise is to produce a penalty which accurately reflects both the seriousness of the offence committed and the offender's ability to pay.

So far as dates are concerned, it should be noted that

the new system of unit fines applies to offences committed from October 1992 onwards and that there may be an
overlap with the old system of fines for a few months as
"old" offences make their way through the courts. This
edition has been written, however, on the basis of the
new system being fully in force. In other respects the law
described is up to date as at September 1992.

Jane Benjamin
September 1992

Contents

Chapter 1

Introduction

Before you begin to read the main parts of this book, there are a few points to note.

1. TERMINOLOGY

There are some legal terms we cannot help mentioning in this book. Most of them are commonly used and readily understood, but to avoid any confusion, here are some explanations:

Acquittal:	The decision of the court that you are not guilty.
Conviction:	The decision of the court that you are guilty; being found guilty.
Defence:	The arguments you use if you decide to dispute the case. Also used to refer to the person defending the case, or his lawyer.
Disqualification:	Being barred from driving – your licence is taken away from you.
Endorsable offence:	An offence for which your driving licence will be marked in some way if you are convicted – you will receive penalty points.
Evidence:	What the witnesses and the police

	have to say about what happened.
Fixed penalty:	A pre-determined punishment for certain kinds of offences; these are explained in Chapter 5.
Magistrates:	The people who hear and decide the case. They are discussed in more detail in Chapter 6.
Mitigation:	If you have been found guilty, or have decided to plead guilty, "mitigation" is the argument, or arguments, you can use to reduce the punishment you might otherwise get.
Penalty points:	Black marks devised to discourage persistent offenders. They are written onto your driving licence. Penalty points are discussed in detail in Chapter 3.
Proceedings:	A general word referring to the train of legal activity.
Prosecution:	The commencement of the legal case against you.
Sentence:	The punishment – a fine, penalty points, disqualification or in extremely serious cases, imprisonment.
Summons:	The piece of paper by which the proceedings are started.
Statement:	Evidence put down in writing.
Witness:	A person (including a police officer) who saw the incident in question.

2. CALLING THE POLICE TO THE SCENE OF AN ACCIDENT

There are some circumstances in which the police *must* be notified of an accident and these are explained later in the book (please see page 38), but the police are not *required* to become involved in every collision. In many cases, provided that names, addresses and registration numbers (and preferably insurance details also) are exchanged between the drivers, they may go their own separate ways without the constabulary being troubled.

Some motorists will insist that the police are called to the scene of an accident. Occasionally this can be counter-productive and it has been known for a motorist, convinced he is blameless, to insist that the police are called, only to find it is he (or indeed she) who is subsequently prosecuted. If you believe that your driving is capable of being criticised, it might be prudent to exchange the relevant particulars with the other driver and then leave it to the insurance companies to decide between themselves who was at fault.

If the police are called to the scene it is likely that they will ask you to explain what happened and make a statement. You should remember that anything said to a police officer is likely to be recorded by him in his notebook, either at the time it is said, or subsequently. Any statement made can be referred to later if proceedings are commenced. Something said on the spur of the moment may be regretted later, but by then it is too late to retract. You should, therefore, think very carefully before you speak to a police officer, and, if pressed for a statement, it might be wise to write it out for yourself, since then you will only say what you want to be said and in the way you wish it to be expressed. There is no obligation on you to make a statement, and if you are in doubt, say nothing.

3. AVOIDING PROSECUTION

It is usually the police who begin legal proceedings against motorists, although occasionally they may be brought by a local authority. If proceedings are to be commenced against you, it is likely that you will be warned first, either orally or in writing. In many cases the old "notice of intended prosecution" is no longer required. However, if proceedings *are* to be brought, the police must bring them within six months of the incident in question, except in the most exceptional instances.

If you have received a warning that you might be prosecuted it is sometimes worthwhile writing to the Chief Constable expressing your regret for the offence, offering your assurances that you will be more vigilant in the future and generally showing your concern to be the perfect motorist. In some minor cases this *may* work to avoid the matter being taken any further, but it is not guaranteed, and the more serious the incident the less likely it is that such a letter will have the desired effect.

It frequently happens that a motorist is charged with *two* offences following the same incident. If, for example, you were charged with careless driving *and* another less serious offence arising out of the same set of circumstances, it might be possible to reach a compromise with the police whereby the less serious matter will be dropped if you plead Guilty to careless driving. Again, it is common for an accusation of driving without due care and attention to be coupled with an allegation of failure to comply with a give way or stop sign. In reality, the motorist may have obeyed the sign and then proceeded forward in the honest but mistaken belief that the road was clear, only to become involved in an accident with another vehicle. Sometimes an offer to plead Guilty to careless driving on the basis that the other charge will be withdrawn will meet with the agreement of the police. Unfortunately this tends not to work the other way round – you are extremely unlikely to be able to persuade the police to drop the more serious charge and proceed with the lesser one alone.

Most, if not all, police forces now operate what is called a "vehicle defect rectification scheme". Under this scheme, if you are stopped driving a vehicle which is defective you may be given a notice telling you that if you have the vehicle satisfactorily repaired (or scrapped!) and produce proof of that fact within 14 days, you can avoid prosecution. If you do not comply with these requirements, however, a prosecution will be launched against you in the usual way.

4. SOLICITORS

If you are charged with a serious motoring offence, or intend to plead Not Guilty, it is prudent to seek at least the preliminary advice of a solicitor. He or she should be able to ascertain the nature of the police evidence and to advise you on your prospects of success. It is pointless to fight a hopeless cause, because, following conviction you may well be required to pay the prosecution costs and witnesses' expenses in addition to the fine. If the prospects are bleak, you may be able to reduce your financial loss by pleading Guilty. More is said on this subject in Chapter 7.

5. PUNISHMENTS

Penalty points are awarded for most motoring offences. The numbers of points awarded for individual motoring offences are set out in the Table on page 119 and the penalty points system is explained in detail in Chapter 3. A motorist who collects 12 or more penalty points within a period of three years risks being disqualified for at least six months.

Ever since the dawn of the motoring age, the most common form of punishment for the erring motorist has been the fine. Many people, however, have complained for many years that fines for motoring offences have been:
• too heavy for people of average or low means;
• meaningless to the rich;
• inconsistent from one area to another.
In order to try and make the fine a fairer punishment across the board, the law was changed in October 1992 to introduce what is known as the "unit fine" system. Instead of thinking directly in terms of money, magistrates now have to assess the seriousness of an offence in units on a scale from 1 to 50 and then multiply that number by the offender's "disposable weekly income" to create the unit fine.

The "disposable weekly income" figure is arrived at by use of a formula as follows:

$$\frac{I - E}{3}$$

where "I" is the offender's weekly income and "E" is his or her allowable expenditure according to official rules. Since it is recognised that most people's expenditure tends to rise with their income, the division by three ensures that only a third of the offender's "spare" income can be got at. Since magistrates' powers are not limitless, the rules also provide that the maximum disposable weekly income figure is £100, so that the highest possible fine is £5,000 (50 units at £100 each). At the other end of the scale the minimum disposable weekly income figure is £4, so the lowest possible fine is also £4 (1 unit at £4).

Although the law fixes maximum fines, these top rates are fairly rarely imposed. Throughout the book you will find information about the maximum fine and the "usual" unit fine for various offences. The maximum fine is arrived at by multiplying the maximum number of units which the law says can be imposed for the offence by the maximum disposable weekly income figure (presently £100). So far as the "usual" unit fines are concerned, it is important to bear in mind that these are only an indication of what is likely to happen. The magistrates will decide in each case exactly what number of units they think most appropriate and in reaching that decision they must take into account first and foremost the *seriousness of the offence*.

The number of units quoted as the "usual unit fine" or the unit fine "which can be expected" are based on an average offence of the kind in question coupled with a timely guilty plea and no "aggravating" factors (things like deliberately bad driving, excessive speed, excess alcohol or drugs etc). They are a broad guide only and in any one individual case many factors are taken into account which could result in a quite different level of unit fine. Furthermore, when the offence is dealt with under the fixed penalty procedure (explained in Chapter 5), there is no appearance in Court and the amount of the fine is fixed, so that references to a "usual unit fine" do not apply.

Chapter 2

Common motoring offences

It is important to note that in this chapter references are made to the fixed penalty procedure, which is explained in Chapter 5. Where this procedure applies, the amount of the fine is pre-determined (£40 if the offence is endorsable; £20 if it is not), so that information given here about the "usual fine" or the fine "that can be expected" will be appropriate only if you are summonsed to appear before a Court, and not where you have merely been given a "ticket".

It should also be noted that as a result of a change in the law in July 1992, police forces are now able to install camera equipment at various places for the automatic detection of speeding and traffic light offences. The camera will photograph the offending vehicle so that it can be identified by its number plate; it will also produce a record of the speed of the vehicle if a speeding offence is alleged, or will show its position relative to the traffic lights in the case of a traffic light offence. Although the camera which records traffic light infringements will be installed in a fixed position at such lights, cameras for detecting speeding offences may well be mobile and mounted on patrol cars. The photographs produced by the devices will be able to be used as evidence in court.

Having identified the offending vehicle by its number plate, the police, if they wish to bring the matter to Court, will first send a notice to the person recorded by the DVLC computer as the keeper of the vehicle. That notice will require the keeper to identify the driver of the vehicle at the relevant time. As a disincentive to throwing it in the bin, the new law says that failure to provide the necessary information is itself an offence which will result in the endorsement of 3 penalty points on the keeper's own driving licence!

1. DRIVING LICENCES

You may not drive a motor vehicle on a public road unless you have a driving licence. The licence must be in force at the time of driving and must apply to the sort of vehicle being used. If you drive a vehicle without the appropriate licence (or rather, "otherwise than in accordance with" a licence as the law now puts it), you are at risk of being fined up to £1,000, although normally you could expect to receive a fine in the region of 5 units. In addition, in many cases, the Driver and Vehicle Licensing Centre at Swansea will be notified, and between 3 and 6 penalty points will be registered on any licence that you apply for in the future. The fixed penalty procedure (see Chapter 5) may be used; if it is, only 3 penalty points will be recorded against you.

There are two types of standard driving licence – *provisional* and *full*. Both are usually valid until you reach 70 years of age, except for a provisional licence restricted to the use of motor cycles only. Although a provisional licence valid to age 70 for a learner aged 17 suggests either pessimism or dedication (!), a provisional licence restricted to motor cycles only is valid for just 2 years and may not be renewed until an interval of at least 12 months has elapsed since it expired. If you pass the two part motor cycle test within the 2 years that the provisional licence is valid, then that licence may be exchanged for a full licence to ride motor cycles.

Restrictions may be imposed on your driving licence if

you suffer from a physical disability such as epilepsy or defective eyesight which cannot be corrected by glasses. The restriction may take the form of limiting the types of vehicle you may drive, or limiting the duration of your licence. If you fall victim to such a disability and it is likely to persist for more than 3 months, you must inform the Driver and Vehicle Licensing Centre at Swansea.

Minimum age limits are imposed before you may drive and these vary according to the vehicle. You must be at least 16 before you may ride a motor cycle and 17 before you may drive a car or similar vehicle. A minimum age of 21 must be reached before you are allowed to drive a large goods or passenger carrying vehicle, although there are some limited exceptions to this. If you have reached 70 years of age, a driving licence may be renewed for periods of three years at a time.

If you hold a provisional licence you are required to comply with certain restrictions:

- you must display "L" plates;
- you may not drive a motor car or similar vehicle without being supervised by a qualified driver sitting in the front passenger seat; a "qualified" driver is someone who has a full driving licence to drive that sort of vehicle, although he or she need not necessarily have been specially trained to teach others to drive;
- you may not ride a motor cycle above 125 c.c. or carry a pillion passenger unless that person has himself passed the motor cycle test;
- you may not drive on a motorway; and
- you may not drive a vehicle when it is towing a trailer.

If you fail to comply with any of these restrictions you could receive a fine of up to £1,000 for driving "otherwise than in accordance with a licence", although a fine of approximately 4 units is more likely. In addition, between 3 and 6 penalty points would be registered on your driving licence. The fixed penalty procedure (see Chapter 5) may be used; if it is, only 3 penalty points will be recorded against you.

If you have a full licence, then you may drive without

restriction vehicles for which you have passed a test. Note that if you have passed a test in a car with automatic transmission, your licence will permit you to drive automatics only, not manuals. With a full licence, you may also drive vehicles for which you have not yet passed a test (except a motor cycle of over 125 c.c.), but you must comply with all the age requirements and other restrictions applicable to provisional licence holders, which are set out above. For example, if you have a licence to drive a motor car, then you may ride a moped (which is a motor cycle with an engine capacity not more than 50 c.c. and is frequently equipped with pedals or is designed for a maximum speed of 30 m.p.h.); and you may even ride a motor cycle of up to 125 c.c. as long as you display "L" plates, avoid the motorways and do not carry a pillion passenger. If you do not comply with any of these requirements or restrictions, you will be liable to the same financial punishments and penalty points as if you were a provisional licence holder.

You must sign your licence and notify the Driver and Vehicle Licensing Centre at Swansea of any change of name or address. Failure to do so is punishable with a maximum fine of £1,000 although a nominal unit fine is usually imposed.

If a police officer requires you to produce your driving licence you must do so personally at the time of the request, or within 7 days at a police station of your choice. The procedure for doing this is explained in more detail on page 40. The problems which are usually encountered in connection with driving licences can frequently be resolved by answering two simple questions:

• Did you have a licence at the time in question, and, if so,

• Did it cover you to drive the type of vehicle concerned? If you drive a vehicle without any licence at all you have no excuse whatever and you will not escape conviction. If you do have a licence but it does not apply to the sort of vehicle you were driving, then once again there is no alternative but to plead Guilty. If you are unsure about the types of vehicle you may drive, then consult your driving licence – an explanation is given on the rear.

Occasionally you may be asked to give a friend or relative a driving lesson. It would be wise to insist on seeing their driving licence before agreeing to do so. If you fail to take that precaution, and later it becomes clear that the learner driver does not have a licence, you risk being prosecuted for permitting him or her to drive without one, even though you did not know that was the case. Upon conviction, you will be fined although your own licence cannot be endorsed with penalty points. If you *were* aware from the outset that the learner driver did not have a licence, then you will be convicted of "aiding and abetting" the offence, which will attract between 3 and 6 penalty points on your licence. It is also prudent to ensure that the required "L" plates are on the car when giving a driving lesson, otherwise your own licence may be endorsed with 3 – 6 penalty points if it can be shown that they were not displayed and you knew they were not.

A motorist who drives without a licence may also be liable to prosecution for driving without insurance. This follows because many insurance policies contain a condition that the policy will only be effective if the driver holds a licence and has not been disqualified.

There are some motorists who have little respect for the law and continue to drive despite the fact that they have lost their licences by disqualification either as a result of a conviction for drinking and driving or by virtue of having accumulated 12 penalty points. As might be expected the Courts impose very heavy financial punishments on such individuals, almost inevitably extend the period of disqualification, and will not infrequently send the motorist to prison.

2. INSURANCE

Before you are entitled to use a motor vehicle on a public

road, you must be insured. "Use" includes not only driving, but also leaving your vehicle on the road, even when it is incapable of being driven because it has broken down or is awaiting repair.

If you are not insured, you can expect very little sympathy from a Court, who will view such a matter very seriously indeed. Magistrates are well aware that if a driver is not insured, other quite innocent people who are injured or who have their property damaged may not be able to recover any compensation. As a consequence, heavy fines and a substantial number of penalty points are imposed. The maximum fine is £5,000 and between 6 and 8 penalty points could be registered on your driving licence. If your lack of insurance was the result of a genuine mistake, you can expect a fine in the region of 15 units, but if it was deliberate, a fine well in excess of this may be imposed, together with 7 or 8 penalty points if you are lucky enough to escape disqualification.

It is your obligation to make certain that you are insured. Fortunately, most insurance brokers and companies send out reminders when the time for renewal is close. However, you should not rely entirely on this, especially if you have moved address in the last 12 months. If you genuinely forgot to renew your insurance policy and it expired shortly before the offence was committed, you can expect a certain amount of leniency, but you are nevertheless Guilty of driving without insurance.

There is only one way of escaping conviction for a charge of driving without insurance, but its scope is very limited. It concerns a person who is driving his employer's vehicle while working for that employer and where the obligation is on the employer to take out the insurance. Provided the driver honestly believed that he was insured, he cannot be convicted.

If you are required by a police officer to produce your insurance, it is only the insurance certificate or cover note, not the whole policy, that he is interested in seeing. This must be produced personally, either there and then, or within 7 days at a police station of your choice. The procedure for doing this is explained more fully on page 40. Sometimes, large companies have made arrangements with the police for the employer to produce the insurance details to a nominated police station.

Mistakes concerning insurance are frequently made when a motorist borrows someone else's vehicle. The law requires that the driver must be insured to drive, either under his or her own policy, or under the policy of the owner of the vehicle. This is an "absolute" obligation, which means that there is *no* excuse for failure.

If you wish to borrow a friend's or relative's car, then you should make certain that you are insured to drive it. If you fail to check, you are at risk of being prosecuted if it transpires that you are not insured. If you lend your vehicle to someone else you should take similar precautions. A failure to do so might result in prosecution against *you*, for permitting the driver to use the vehicle without insurance. As a consequence, you will be fined and penalty points imposed on your licence. In addition, should the motorist become involved in an accident, it is unlikely that your insurance company would be interested in paying for the cost of repairs. Clearly, lending your car to someone else without checking the insurance could prove an extremely costly favour!

As already mentioned, a motorist who does not have a driving licence, or who has been disqualified, is likely to be prosecuted for driving without insurance, even if a policy has been taken out for that vehicle. This flows from the fact that most insurance policies stipulate that the insurance is effective only if the driver holds a licence and has not been disqualified.

Driving without insurance or permitting someone else to do so is an offence which carries a variable number of penalty points, enabling the Court to reflect its attitude to the offence and the offender when selecting the number of points to impose. In a genuine case where, unknown to the motorist, a policy of insurance expired shortly before the offence in question, it may be possible to persuade the Court to award the minimum, which is 6 points.

Where the Court feels the motorist has been lax, 7 or 8 points are more likely, and where the offence was deliberate then disqualification is often imposed or if it is not, 7 or 8 points are almost certain. In the same way the level of the unit fine will reflect whether the offence was committed deliberately or inadvertently.

3. MOT AND TAX DISC

Every motor vehicle which is 3 or more years old is required to pass a Ministry of Transport test, and if successful, an "MOT" certificate will be issued and this is valid for 12 months. Should you drive a vehicle without the necessary certificate, you may be prosecuted. The maximum fine is £1,000, but it is suggested that 3 units are likely to be imposed, especially where the MOT certificate is less than 3 months out of date. The offence is not "endorsable" and therefore no penalty points can be placed on your licence. There is only one way to escape conviction in such a case – if you can prove that you were on your way to, or from, the nearest convenient MOT testing station you cannot be convicted. So if your MOT has actually run out, it is wise to pre-book the test before setting off, so that if you are stopped, the garage can confirm you were on your way there.

Every motor vehicle which is being used, or is allowed to stand, on the road must have and display a current excise licence, commonly referred to as a tax disc. The owner or driver of a vehicle who is in breach of this regulation could be liable to a hefty fine. The unit fine system does not apply to excise offences, and the maximum fine is £1,000 or 5 times the annual rate of duty payable, whichever is the greater. However, the usual fine is twice the duty lost, and a claim can be made for back duty if this has not been paid before the Court hearing.

Again, there is only one escape route – where the vehicle is 3 or more years old, and you can prove that you were on your way directly to, or from, the nearest convenient MOT testing station. This is an acceptable explanation because you cannot obtain a tax disc unless you are able to produce a current MOT certificate. Here also, it would be wise to have pre-booked your motor car into the garage.

Although a tax disc may be in force for the vehicle concerned, it is an offence if it is not properly displayed. In the case of a car, the disc should be fixed to the nearside of the front windscreen. If you have a valid tax disc but it is not displayed, the maximum fine is £200; if it has merely fallen from the windscreen then a relatively modest unit fine would be imposed or, in certain circumstances, an absolute discharge (which means no punishment is imposed) may be granted. Alternatively, this offence may be dealt with by way of a fixed penalty (see Chapter 5).

Occasionally motorists get themselves into serious trouble by transferring the tax disc from one motor vehicle to another. This is a fraudulent use of the tax disc and is regarded very severely; it carries a maximum fine of £5,000. The excuse often put forward is that the disc was transferred inadvertently rather than deliberately. Although mistakes of this nature may sometimes occur, a Court will require a lot of convincing before it accepts such an explanation.

4. ROADWORTHY CONDITION

Every motor vehicle used on a public road must be in a roadworthy condition. Whether or not a vehicle meets those conditions is determined by a set of Rules known as the Motor Vehicle (Construction and Use) Regulations, made in 1986. These Regulations create scores of possible offences, which vary from having a vehicle in a state where it could be described as a "mobile deathtrap" to having no water in your windscreen washer bottle. It is impossible in a short book of this nature to mention all the potential offences, and so the discussion is confined to the few most important ones – tyres, steering, brakes, and "dangerous condition". Three penalty points may be imposed for an offence in connection with any of these. The other offences, which are not mentioned here, are less serious and are usually dealt with by way of a modest unit fine.

The law requires that every part of the braking system of a motor vehicle must be in an efficient working order. If the brakes do not work, or if there is excess travel in the handbrake or foot brake, that is an offence. Whether or not it is true that your brakes do not work, or have excess travel, is a question of the facts. If you are prosecuted, it is likely that a police officer will complain that he found the brakes to be defective for one reason or another. When a police officer inspects your vehicle in the first place he will inform you of his findings. It would then be wise to have your vehicle inspected by a garage immediately, to discover whether or not the police account of the matter is correct. Should the garage disagree with the police officer, you could rely on the garage as a witness and require them to give evidence in your favour. How this is done is explained in more detail in Chapter 6.

Similar provisions apply to the steering. Any play which is found in the steering, however small, will render it defective. Once again, if you disagree with the police officer, you should have the vehicle inspected by a garage immediately.

Every tyre, including the spare, is required to have at least 1.6 mm of tread in a continuous band all the way round the circumference, and across the central three-quarters of the breadth of the tread. If this is not the case, the tyre is defective. It is also defective if it has a hole, rip or bulge. If you do not agree with the police officer, you should have the tyre inspected by an appropriate manufacturer who will provide a report for a fee. There is no obligation to carry a spare wheel and it would be unwise to have a defective spare because you can be prosecuted even though that tyre was not in use. Note also that *each* tyre found to be defective amounts to a separate offence.

All motor vehicles must be in such a condition that they will not cause danger to any member of the public, however remote. Sometimes a prosecution will say that a vehicle is in a defective condition because there are sharp edges on the body work. If your vehicle has been involved in a collision causing sharp points in the metal work, it is a good idea to mask them over until they can be repaired properly, even though an injury could only be caused to a pedestrian by their rubbing themselves along the side of your vehicle.

All these "construction and use" offences can be dealt with by a fixed penalty (see Chapter 5). If not, the maximum fine for a vehicle which has defective brakes, steering or tyres, or is in a dangerous condition, is £2,500 although normally a fine in the region of 4 units will be imposed for each offence. In addition to a fine, 3 penalty points will be awarded.

Before leaving the subject of the maintenance and condition of your vehicle, a few words about some of the other hazards would be appropriate. The offences listed in the rest of this section are not endorsable and are normally dealt with by a modest fine, except for the offences of unsafe load, overloading or carrying an excessive number of passengers.

It is essential that you keep your windows, windscreen wipers and washers, and mirrors clean, unobstructed and in efficient working order. You should not plaster your rear windscreen with stickers or allow your windows to become so dirty that it is difficult to see through them. In winter you should clear the ice or snow from all your windows, not just a small area of the front windscreen.

If your windscreen wipers do not clear the windscreen properly then they are defective and an offence has been committed. If your washer bottle runs out of water that too is an offence but it is extremely doubtful that you would be prosecuted if it had merely frozen up. Your vehicle must be fitted with mirrors and in modern vehicles this includes an internal and an outside mirror. You are not entitled to "pile up" luggage so that you cannot see out of your rear view mirror unless you are driving a van or an estate car which has a nearside mirror. You must also be able to see in your mirrors. If they are cracked, dirty or worn out then an offence has been committed. It is often wise to go to the expense of having a nearside mirror fitted, especially if you do a lot of driving in built-up areas.

If you carry anything on a roof rack it must be securely fixed because, if it comes off, you run the risk of being prosecuted for having an unsafe load. It does not matter that you have taken some precautions because all the prosecution have to prove is that something came adrift. If you overload your vehicle so that it exceeds the permitted weight an offence is committed, and if you carry too many passengers you are also at risk of prosecution. For offences of unsafe load, overloading or carrying too many passengers you will get 3 penalty points and a fine of 6 units is likely to be imposed, unless a fixed penalty is given (see Chapter 5).

If you leave your vehicle you are required to switch off your engine and apply the handbrake. Finally, it is illegal to sell a motor vehicle which is not in a roadworthy condition unless it was a "term of the sale" that the vehicle would not be used on a road until the defects were rectified.

5. SPEEDING

The most common offence committed by motorists is exceeding the speed limit.

Unless there are signs indicating otherwise, a maximum speed of 30 m.p.h. applies to all roads where the street lighting columns are less than 200 yards apart. In addition, local highway authorities may impose a 30 m.p.h. limit even if there is no such system of street lighting, but such a limit will be signposted. It is therefore prudent to travel no faster than 30 m.p.h. in a built-up area unless it is clear that a higher limit applies.

On "de-restricted" roads the maximum speed is 60 m.p.h. on a single carriageway or 70 m.p.h. on a dual carriageway.

Temporary speed limits may be imposed on any road, including a motorway, where there are road works and signs displayed. The maximum speed on a motorway is 70 m.p.h. although on certain stretches of urban motorways the limits may be 50 m.p.h. or 60 m.p.h., which will be signposted. Temporary recommended speed signs may be displayed on motorways in hazardous road conditions or following an accident. While it is wise to obey these, it is not an offence in itself if you do not. However, if you become involved in an accident as a consequence of travelling faster than a recommended speed, it could amount to careless driving.

Certain experiments are being conducted by the Department of Transport in connection with motorway speed limits whereby a legal maximum speed is imposed at some road works. Warning is given by signs telling drivers that they are approaching a mandatory speed restriction area and the speed restriction signs are exactly the same as those which you now see on a non-motorway road – a circular sign bordered with red. Breach of such limits is an offence which carries 3-6 penalty points.

Lower speed limits are imposed on certain *vehicles* irrespective of the maximum speed limit for the *road* in question. Among these is a limit of 50 m.p.h. when towing a trailer (60 m.p.h. on a motorway or dual carriageway).

The police use many weird and wonderful devices to detect whether you are travelling faster than you should be. Whichever method is relied on, a Court will require very solid proof from you before they will reject a police officer's statement of your speed.

The most controversial method used to calculate a motorist's speed is the radar speed gun. As a result of certain court cases, some police forces withdrew them from use. They are susceptible to interference from radio signals or large objects such as road signs, either of which could cause a false reading. However, the instructions for the use of the gun have been improved to ensure correct readings, and unless you could prove that the gun was improperly used, the Court would almost certainly accept its reading of your speed.

Another method used by the police is "Vascar". This is used in a police vehicle equipped with a small computer. The police vehicle is driven over a measured distance which is then recorded into the machine. When a motorist travels across the first point of reference the clock is started and when he passes across the second point, it is stopped. The machine then calculates the average speed. These devices can be extremely accurate and the training given to police officers enables them to calculate a vehicle's speed to within 1 m.p.h..

It may happen that, while accepting you have exceeded the speed limit, you disagree with the estimate of your actual speed put forward by the police. As the technical devices such as a radar speed trap or gun produce an accurate result, any dispute as to your actual speed is likely to arise only where the police reckoning of your speed is based on their having followed you. If you find yourself in this situation then the plea should be one of Guilty, and you should notify the police of your intention to give evidence at the hearing as to your actual speed. It is then up to the police to arrange for the police officer to be in Court to give his side of the story and argue the case. If they do not take that step, you could end up with a lesser fine.

As a matter of interest, a prosecution for speeding is not usually brought unless you have been discovered driving at least 10 m.p.h. over the limit.

Speeding offences may be dealt with by a fixed penalty of £40 and 3 penalty points (see Chapter 5), but if you were very much over the speed limit it may well be that you will be prosecuted instead. If that happens, and you are convicted, the amount of the unit fine and the number of penalty points will depend on by how much you exceeded the limit. For example, if you exceed the limit by less than 30 m.p.h., the usual penalty will be between 3 and 6 units and your licence will be endorsed with between 3 and 6 points. If, however, you exceed the limit by more than 30 m.p.h. you face a likely fine of 7 or 8 units and there is a serious risk of your being disqualified for a short period.

6. PEDESTRIAN CROSSINGS, TRAFFIC LIGHTS AND ROAD SIGNS

Each time you approach a pedestrian crossing, a set of traffic lights or an obligatory road sign (and you can recognise an obligatory road sign by the red border, indicating that you *must* obey it) you should exercise considerable care. Each of these obstacles is dealt with in turn below.

There are two types of pedestrian crossing – zebra and pelican. Fortunately, zebra crossings are being phased out and replaced by the safer pelican variety, which should be treated in much the same way as a set of traffic lights. Here, the flashing amber signal means that you may only move forward if there are no pedestrians using, or about to use, the crossing.

At a zebra crossing the pedestrian has the right of way. If he or she puts a foot on any part of the black and white markings before you actually reach those markings you are legally obliged to stop, even if it would be a physical impossibility to do so. Fortunately, the police take a realistic view. They would be unlikely to prosecute a motorist who failed to stop having been merely inches away from the crossing when a pedestrian ran into it without paying any regard for his or her own safety. A prosecution would follow, however, if a pedestrian was well established on the crossing and you had ample opportunity to stop before reaching it.

A zebra crossing which has a central reservation or island in the middle of it can be treated as if it were two separate crossings. You are then only obliged to watch out for your half of the crossing.

Failure to give way to a pedestrian on a crossing of either type is an offence which can attract a maximum fine of £1,000. In reality a fine of approximately 3 units might be expected, but in addition 3 penalty points will be endorsed on your driving licence.

You will find that both before and after a zebra crossing there are zig-zag lines marked on the road. It is an offence to overtake a motor vehicle within the area of the zig-zag lines *before* the crossing, although you are permitted to overtake *after* the crossing itself. An offence of this nature is punishable by a maximum fine of £1,000, but usually 3 units will be ordered, and there are 3 penalty points.

It is also an offence to park anywhere within the zig-zag lines, either before or after the crossing; this amounts to parking a vehicle in a dangerous position as it obstructs other drivers' vision of the crossing. A fixed penalty is a possibility (see Chapter 5), but if you are prosecuted the offence will usually attract a fine of approximately 3 units and 3 penalty points.

When you approach a set of traffic lights you can never be certain whether they will remain green in your favour, or turn to red before you reach them. Parliament recognised this obvious difficulty and incorporated the amber signal. Amber means stop, unless unsafe to do so, although many motorists wrongly treat it in much the same way as a green signal. There is a 3 second interval between the green and red signals, and this ought to give every motorist ample opportunity to slow down and come to a stop before reaching the line, or alternatively, if too close to stop they should have passed well across the junction within the 3 seconds before the lights change to red.

It is not an offence in itself to cross the stop line when the lights are amber, but if you are subsequently involved in a collision you may be prosecuted for driving without due care and attention. Failure to comply with traffic lights is an offence which attracts a maximum fine of £1,000, although normally a fine in the region of 3 units is imposed. In addition, 3 penalty points will be endorsed on your licence. Again, there is the alternative of a fixed penalty of £40 (see Chapter 5).

Where there is no accident but a prosecution is brought against the motorist for failure to comply with a traffic light, the incident is normally witnessed by police officers who follow and stop the offending motorist. This often makes it difficult to avoid conviction because the Court will fairly readily accept the evidence of one or more police officers. The only argument which may be effective will be that the police officers were too far away from the junction to be able to determine whether you crossed the stop line on red or amber.

"Road signs" include posts in the ground to which signs are attached and also white lines painted on the road surface. All signs should be obeyed, but the punishment for disobedience is greater in some circumstances than in others. Failure to comply with a "Stop" sign is punishable with a maximum fine of £1,000 although normally about 3 units will be imposed. Unfortunately 3 penalty points would also be added to your driving licence. Non-compliance with a "Give way", "No entry" or "Keep left" sign is likely to be punishable with the same financial penalty, but no points would be awarded. Again, both offences – failing to stop and failing to comply – may be subject to fixed penalties as an alternative to prosecution.

Failure to comply with the double white lines, however, is subject to 3 penalty points. The rule is that you may not cross the centre lines where there are two solid white lines, or where there is a solid white line on your side of the road and a broken white line on the other.

You may escape conviction for crossing double white lines if you can prove to the court that it was necessary to do so in order to turn into a sideroad or onto land which adjoins the highway, to pass a stationary vehicle or to avoid an accident; or that you did so in circumstances beyond your control. However, the motorist who is in the process of overtaking slower moving vehicles and then encounters an area of double white lines may not get the sympathy of a Court because he is likely to have had some advance warning before reaching the restricted area. Apart from crossing double white lines it is also an offence to stop on an area of road marked with double white lines, even if one line only is solid and is not on your side of the road.

It is also an offence to drive on areas of hatched markings but in this instance, a conviction is not endorsable.

7. CARELESS DRIVING

Driving without due care and attention and driving without reasonable consideration for other road users are commonly referred to together as "careless driving". A motorist who was responsible for an accident or almost caused an accident is often charged with one or other of these offences. The charge of careless driving amounts to a criticism of your driving on the particular occasion.

The standard by which a court judges our driving is that of the near-perfect motorist – in lawyer's language, you are expected to be "reasonable, competent and prudent"! Since none of us is perfect we are all at a greater or lesser risk of being prosecuted for careless driving. The Magistrates' Court will hear what the witnesses have to say, and then consider whether or not the motorist came up to scratch. Each particular case is determined according to its own facts, and the result in one case does not mean that the outcome will be the same in a similar case.

Unlike many other legal procedures, the Magistrates' Court hearing a motoring offence is not concerned with assessing the *degree* of responsibility of the motorist. Technically, a Magistrates' Court can convict a motorist if convinced he was as little as 1% to blame. Fortunately, a more practical approach is adopted. The police do not normally bring proceedings for careless driving unless there is independent evidence from witnesses who saw the incident to indicate that the motorist is Guilty, or the circumstances of the accident speak for themselves.

There are some obvious instances of careless driving:

- It is difficult to justify running into the back of the motorist in front of you;
- If you pull out of a side road and are in collision with a vehicle on a major road you are likely to be at fault;
- If you turn right across the path of an approaching motorist who is then in collision with you, again it is likely that you will be convicted.

However, many allegations of careless driving are not so clear cut. You should ask yourself whether you did something which could be considered foolish, or had you taken every precaution to ensure that your manoeuvre could be carried out in complete safety? If you are still uncertain, it might be wise to consult a solicitor, who should be able to obtain the police version of the incident. The solicitor can then advise you on your prospects of success. In coming to a conclusion, however, it is important to distinguish between those factors which might establish that you are Not Guilty at all; and those which can be used to show that although Guilty, there was a relatively low degree of carelessness and that therefore the court should be lenient in fixing the punishment.

The maximum fine for the careless driving offences is £2,500, but a straightforward case is likely to result in a fine of 6 units. In addition, a variable number of penalty points, between 3 and 9, will be awarded. However, this fine, and the number of penalty points, can vary considerably according to the circumstances. In assessing the punishment, it is the extent of the carelessness that is important, and not the consequences of the incident. A trivial case may be dealt with lightly, but high unit fines will be imposed if you have been extremely careless.

8. DANGEROUS DRIVING; CAUSING DEATH BY DANGEROUS DRIVING

Offences of dangerous driving or causing death by dangerous driving are extremely serious. Under no circumstances should you attempt to deal with these matters without the advice and help of a solicitor. If you face such a charge, then almost certainly your insurance company will provide legal representation at their expense. If not, it may well be that you are entitled to legal aid, especially if the allegation is causing death by dangerous driving – a matter which can be dealt with only by the Crown Court.

"Dangerous" in the context of dangerous driving refers to danger either of personal injury or of serious damage to property, and a driver can only be said to be driving dangerously if the way he drives falls *far below* what would be expected of a competent and careful driver, and it would be obvious to such a person that driving in that way would be dangerous. Instances of dangerous driving commonly include driving at a very fast speed in a built-up area, weaving in and out between vehicles or overtaking on a blind bend or on the brow of a hill. It is also possible to commit a dangerous driving offence by merely driving a vehicle if its condition is such that it would be obvious that driving it in its current state would be dangerous!

The difference between "dangerous" and "careless" driving is often a matter of degree. Dangerous requires an obvious risk, whereas in careless driving the risks of injury or damage need not be great. A motorist who, in approaching a set of traffic lights on amber, tries to get across before the red light but fails and is as a consequence involved in an accident is likely to be charged with careless driving. A motorist who approaches a set of traffic lights which have been red for some time, but decides to drive through them anyway, is likely to be charged with dangerous driving since there is a greater risk that a collision will occur.

The Courts attempt to discourage dangerous behaviour on the roads by imposing very heavy fines, disqualification and even imprisonment. If fatal injuries have been caused by dangerous driving, a term of imprisonment is likely to be imposed, especially if excessive speed or alcohol were involved. The maximum fine which a Magistrates' Court may impose for dangerous driving is £5,000, plus disqualification for not less than 12 months, and/or six months imprisonment. The probable penalty is a fine of between 20 and 30 units and disqualification for at least 12 months. The court must also order the motorist to take another driving test – not the usual 'L' test, but an extended test about twice as long which includes driving on unrestricted dual carriageways. If you are convicted of causing death by dangerous driving by the Crown Court, a period of up to 5 years imprisonment may be imposed.

9. FAILURE TO STOP; FAILING TO REPORT AN ACCIDENT

Not every accident needs to be reported to the police. The majority of minor collisions are dealt with between the drivers themselves by simply exchanging particulars as described in the next paragraph. However, although you need not necessarily report the accident to the police, there are a number of other things you *are* required to do and if you fail to do them, a heavy fine and a substantial number of penalty points may result, since clearly the Courts wish to discourage "hit and run" motorists.

If you are involved in a collision with another vehicle, or with any building or other property adjacent to the road and damage is caused to that vehicle or property, or if someone besides yourself is injured, you are obliged to *stop* at the scene of the accident. You must give to any person affected by the accident:
- your name and address;
- the name and address of the owner of the vehicle if that is someone other than yourself; and

- the registration number of your vehicle.

Except where someone other than the driver has been injured, you are not obliged to give the other person your insurance details; but it is wise to do since it may discourage the other person from calling the police.

If you are involved in a collision with an animal – which includes a horse, cow, sheep, pig or dog, but not a cat! – you must stop and if possible exchange particulars with the owner; otherwise you must report the incident to the police.

A motorist who, having been involved in a collision, gets out of his vehicle, examines the damage to his own car and then drives off is guilty of an offence, even though, technically, he stopped. In this instance he failed to exchange particulars. In order to fulfil your obligation you are required to make reasonable enquiries to discover who is the owner of the damaged property or driver of the vehicle. It is not sufficient to have a quick look round to see if anybody is about and then drive off.

If you collide with a parked car and cannot locate the driver, it is often wise to write out the relevant details on a piece of paper, and fix it to the windscreen wiper. When the owner returns to the vehicle he may then be more inclined to contact *you* than the police. However, even if you have left a note on the windscreen, you are still obliged to report the matter to the police because you have not been able to exchange details with the other driver personally.

If for some reason you are unable to provide your particulars immediately following a collision, then you are obliged to report the accident to the police as soon as is "reasonably practicable", and in any event, within 24 hours. It has long since been decided that a motorist does not automatically have the whole 24 hours in which to report an accident. You must go to the nearest police station *as soon as possible.* Convictions for failing to report have occurred, even when the motorist has been to the police station a few hours after an incident.

If, while driving, you have been involved in an accident

in which someone besides yourself has been hurt, then you are obliged to report the accident to the police as soon as possible, even if you have exchanged names and addresses. The only exception to this is that you need not report the accident if you were able to, and did, produce your certificate of insurance to the injured person at the scene. Otherwise, the accident must be reported to the police or to a police constable immediately, and you must produce your certificate of insurance to a police station within 7 days; the procedure for doing this is explained on page 41.

It is the driver himself or herself who must report the accident – you may not get someone else to do it for you. The details of the accident must be reported to a police station or to a police constable. In the latter case, however, the constable is likely to refer you to a police station.

You may successfully avoid a conviction for an offence of failing to stop, or failing to report an accident, if you can convince the Court that you were not aware that you had been involved in a collision. The test is whether you "knew, or ought reasonably to have known" that you had been involved in that accident. Clearly, this defence is fairly easily available to the drivers of large and heavy vehicles such as lorries or large vans where the extent of the damage is minor; for example, the driver may well not have realised that his tail scraped a car in the next lane. It is more difficult to succeed with this defence when driving a motor car or where the damage is substantial.

The maximum penalty for failing to stop after an accident is £5,000 and/or 6 months imprisonment. Upon conviction you could expect a fine of about 10 units and, depending on the seriousness of the circumstances, the penalty points that will be endorsed on your licence will be between 5 and 10. If it is suspected that alcohol was the main reason for failing to stop, a period of disqualification may be imposed.

The maximum penalty for failing to report an accident is also £5,000 and/or 6 months imprisonment and upon conviction about 10 units can be expected. The range of

points which can be imposed according to the seriousness of the offence is between 5 and 10. Where both
offences, failing to stop *and* failing to report, have been
committed together, the Court will in all probability consider disqualifying you for a period.

10. FAILURE TO PRODUCE DOCUMENTS

In the course of your driving career you are likely to be
requested by a police officer to produce your driving documents. This can happen if the police say that you have
committed a road traffic offence, or following a spot
check. Very few motorists carry all their driving documents with them, and if a police officer wishes to see
them he will issue you with a slip of paper known as
HORT 1. Upon this will be written the address of the
police station at which you have elected to show your
papers, the date by which you must do so, and the
papers which are required to be produced.

You must then set about collecting together your documents. Usually you must produce your driving licence,
certificate of insurance, and, where appropriate, your
MOT certificate. If you do not produce these papers to the
chosen police station within 7 days, you commit an
offence for which the maximum fine is £1,000. However,
the courts take a relatively lenient view and the expected
fine is in the region of 2 units for each document not produced. There is, though, a possible defence. If you can
prove that it was not reasonably practicable to produce
the document(s) before the date on which the police
decide to prosecute, you will escape conviction. This
could be the case where your driving licence has been
sent to Swansea for a change of address or for details of a
previous offence to be endorsed; or if you have lost your
insurance certificate and it takes more than 7 days to
obtain a replacement.

If you do not produce your documents, it can sometimes result in a summons being issued claiming, for

example, that you have no driving licence. Such a summons is usually issued "in the alternative", meaning that you are accused either of not having the document(s) in question at all, or that if you did have them, you failed to produce them. As long as you can produce the documents at Court or to the police before such a summons is heard, the prosecution will then only proceed with the matter of your having failed to produce them.

11. PARKING IN A DANGEROUS POSITION AND OBSTRUCTION

Parking your car illegally can sometimes be more serious that merely incurring a ticket. Should you park within the zig-zag lines of a pedestrian crossing, on the brow of a hill, or on a blind bend, this is regarded as leaving your car in a dangerous position; so is failing to set your handbrake properly causing your vehicle to roll down a hill. Parking in a dangerous position can incur a fixed penalty (see Chapter 5) or, if you are prosecuted, a fine of up to £1,000 although normally fines in the region of 2 to 3 units are imposed. In addition, 3 penalty points will be endorsed on your driving licence. However, if your motor vehicle had genuinely broken down and you were unable to move it, that may be sufficient explanation to avoid any penalty being imposed.

Causing an unnecessary obstruction of the highway is a thorny problem in that it is difficult to define. The only way to approach this is by exercise of common sense. Parking your car for hours on end in a busy and narrow shopping street is asking for trouble unless parking there is specifically permitted. Likewise parking your car partly on the pavement and partly on the road forcing pedestrians to walk into the road to pass is likely to bring about a prosecution. It has been known for factory workers to be prosecuted for parking their vehicles in side roads to the annoyance of local residents. The fact that others besides you have parked in a particular place does not excuse you. Fortunately no penalty points may be imposed for obstruction. The maximum fine is £2,500 in many cases and £1,000 in others. Frequently a fine of 2 units is imposed. In certain cases a fixed penalty ticket (see Chapter 5) may be issued.

12. MOTORWAY OFFENCES

Certain driving offences can be committed only on a motorway. For most of these the maximum fine is £2,500 together with 3 penalty points, and, in some cases, disqualification.

If you are on the main carriageway of a motorway and you reverse, you can expect a fine of about 12 units; should you drive in the wrong direction you can expect a fine of around 20 units plus a period of disqualification. If you indulge in either of these activities while on a slip road, the fine is likely to be in the region of 4 to 6 units. If you drive onto the central reservation, the fine is likely to be 6 units and if you drive onto the hard shoulder without lawful excuse you can expect a fine of about 5 units. If you make a "U" turn on the motorway, then a period of disqualification is likely.

If you stop on the hard shoulder of a slip road or the main carriageway, then a fine of between 2 and 4 units is probable, although there are certain circumstances where such stopping is permissible – if your vehicle breaks down or you run out of petrol, oil or water without which your vehicle cannot be used, then you may stop. You may also stop to give assistance to someone else who is in that position.

If you are towing a trailer you may not use the third lane of a motorway, and failure to comply with this can result in a fine of approximately 10 units, and 3 penalty points will be endorsed on your driving licence.

13. LIGHTING YOUR VEHICLE

The circumstances in which you should turn on your lights are not always fully understood. Complicated Regulations have been laid down by Parliament, and if these are broken a prosecution may result. Fortunately in most instances a fixed penalty or a modest unit fine is the outcome. Offences involving the lighting of your vehicle are not endorsable and therefore no penalty points can be awarded.

The required size, shape and position of lights are well known to motor vehicle manufacturers and there is no need to discuss them in this book.

However, there are many offences concerning the *use* of lights, and these often arise through ignorance. Your headlights must each be of the same size and shape, must emit the same colour light, ie white or yellow, and must switch simultaneously to either dip or main beam. They are also required to match, which means they must give out the same strength of light. It occasionally happens that one of your headlights becomes defective; either it does not work at all, or provides only a dipped or only a main beam. Both are offences. Similar provisions apply to rear lights, which must show only red light. If a rear light becomes damaged so there is some white light showing that is also an offence. It is therefore prudent to mask over the damaged area with red tape or plastic.

Your lights are required to be kept in efficient working order and clean. Especially in times of bad weather, dirt will collect on head lamps and it is wise to clean them regularly. You could be surprised at how much brighter they become! You are required to turn on your headlamps, not sidelights, in the hours of darkness when driving your vehicle except where the road in question has street lamps actually illuminated and not more than 200 yards apart, in which case sidelights are sufficient. The number of motorists who insist on driving on sidelights is surprising. It is equally surprising that they are not involved in more accidents, because they cannot see, or be seen, very well.

Dipped headlights should be illuminated during the daytime if visibility is poor, for example, in fog, smoke, heavy rain or spray, snow, dense cloud or other similar conditions which reduce visibility. In the same conditions, though primarily in fog, you may use rear fog lamps if you have them, though not at any other time. You are also required to ensure that your rear number plate is illuminated.

It may be possible to avoid conviction for having a defective light if you can prove that you had taken reasonable precautions to make sure the light in question was working.

Whether or not your lights should be left on after parking will depend very much on where you leave your vehicle. You must leave the side, tail and registration lights illuminated unless your vehicle is left in a designated parking place or it is parked on a road where the speed limit is not greater than 30 m.p.h. and it is facing the correct way with the nearside of the vehicle closest to the kerb. In a "One Way" street it may be parked on either side of the road provided, of course, it is facing in the correct direction. This exception does not apply if your vehicle is left within 10 metres of a road junction, is equipped to carry more than 8 passengers, or is a goods vehicle with an unladen weight of more than 1525 kilogrammes.

If your vehicle is equipped with hazard warning lights you may display these only if you are stationary. It has become fairly common, especially on motorways, to use hazard warning lights to warn vehicles behind of an obstruction ahead. While this is usually done with a view to road safety, it is in fact illegal. Another practice which is commonplace is flashing your lights at another motorist. Sometimes this is interpreted as "I am coming through"; while on other occasions it is taken to mean "You go first". The Highway Code tells you that such action should be interpreted only as a warning, not as a polite (or even impolite) gesture.

14. SEAT BELTS

Subject to the limited exceptions discussed below, it is now compulsory for both the driver and front seat passenger in a moving motor vehicle to wear a seat belt. It is also compulsory for rear seat passengers to wear belts if these are fitted. It is the person without the belt who commits the offence, so if your passenger does not wear a belt, it is he or she who will be prosecuted rather than you. The maximum punishment is a fine of £500; in court you could expect a fine of 2 units, but if you are dealt with under the fixed penalty system (see Chapter 5) the amount to pay would be £20. On these figures a court appearance would appear to offer a discount to someone whose means are at rock bottom and whose "weekly disposable income" (see Chapter 1) is less than £10; unfortunately for such a person, however, the law provides that in these circumstances the actual amount of the fine can be increased to the level of the appropriate fixed penalty! Your driving licence cannot be endorsed with penalty points for this offence.

There is no requirement upon a driver to wear a seat belt while reversing, or, if he is instructing a learner driver, while the learner driver is reversing. In certain circumstances it is possible to obtain an exemption certificate from your GP to confirm that it is medically inadvisable to wear a seat belt. In addition, the drivers of certain types of *vehicle*, such as local delivery vans, are exempt.

Special rules apply to children. Unless you have a reasonable excuse, it is an offence to allow a child under 14 to ride in the front passenger seat unless wearing a seat belt. It is similarly an offence to allow a child under 14 to ride unbelted in the rear of a vehicle equipped with rear seat belts. Over 14, it is the child himself or herself who is responsible. No offence is committed if the reason the child must sit in the front seat is that every other seat is occupied. There are special provisions with regard to babies under 12 months for whom a special child restraint is required, and for older children who are disabled. Children between one and three years inclusive wearing adult seat belts should be seated on a booster cushion. No offence is committed if a child over 12 months is wearing a seat belt with an inertia reel mechanism which has become locked, or where the seat belt has broken while the journey was in progress. In these cases of children under 14, it is the driver who will be prosecuted, and the penalties are as described in the first paragraph of this section.

15. DRINK AND DRIVING OFFENCES

The drink/driving provisions are complex and important and for this reason they have been given a Chapter of their own – Chapter 4.

16. STOLEN VEHICLES

Although offences of stealing vehicles are offences of theft rather than road traffic matters, it seems worthwhile to outline them here briefly, since this type of crime is ever-increasing and it may be helpful to know the position should you be unfortunate enough to be the victim of such an event.

In the first place, a distinction must be drawn between stealing a motor vehicle and taking a vehicle without the owner's consent. To be convicted of theft, there must be an intention of "depriving the owner permanently of his property". This element of the offence will be taken as read if the offender treats the vehicle as if it were his own. If he were to sell the vehicle, change the registration plates or the colour, that would be sufficient evidence of theft. The "joy rider" who "borrows" someone else's car and later abandons it may escape with the lesser offence of "taking a vehicle without the owner's consent" because it might be said that it would be returned to the owner in due course. Someone who allows himself to be carried in a vehicle knowing that it was stolen or "borrowed" will be guilty of an offence even if he was not involved in taking it in the first place.

If the person who took the vehicle genuinely believed that he had lawful authority to do so, or would have had the owner's consent if he had known of the taking and the circumstances in which it was taken, then he has a defence. The passenger who does not find out that the vehicle has been stolen or taken until after he has got into it and is being driven, should seize the first opportunity to get out of the vehicle and if he does so, he has a defence as he was unaware of the theft. But if he "passes up" the opportunity to get out he might be in difficulty.

Punishments for these offences are severe. For theft the maximum punishment which the Magistrates could impose is 6 months imprisonment plus a substantial fine. However, much longer sentences can be imposed by the Crown Court. For taking a vehicle without the owner's consent a Court may impose a fine of up to £5,000 and/or 6 months imprisonment. In normal circumstances, a fine of 12 to 15 units is likely to be imposed and the court will give serious consideration to a prison sentence. The maximum penalties for allowing yourself to be carried are the same, but a fine of 8 to 10 units is more likely.

In April 1992 a new law was passed to try and cope with the rising tide of dangerous and often lethal joyriding in various parts of the country. Called (rather inelegantly) the "Aggravated Vehicle-Taking Act", it provides that where a vehicle which has been taken without consent is driven dangerously and then involved in an accident which causes personal injury or damage to the vehicle or other property, the occupants of the vehicle may be charged with the serious offence of "aggravated vehicle taking". For that offence, up to two years' imprisonment can be imposed at the Crown Court; but if the accident results in a death that maximum period goes up to five years. In either case, a compulsory disqualification of at least 12 months will also be imposed.

Chapter 3

The penalty points system

1. INTRODUCTION

Apart from a term of imprisonment, the ultimate sanction that can be imposed upon an offending motorist is the withdrawal of his driving licence by disqualification. Although technically the court has power to disqualify, and even order that a new driving test must be passed by, any person who is convicted of a single endorsable offence, this very rarely happens unless the offence is one where disqualification *must by law* be imposed, or the circumstances are so grave that the Court considers disqualification is appropriate.

However, those who regularly commit motoring offences are at risk of disqualification under the Penalty Points System, which was first introduced on 1 November 1982. The principle of this system is that a driver who incurs 12 or more penalty points within a period of 3 years will almost certainly be disqualified for a minimum of 6 months. The intention is to punish a persistent offender, and disqualification will be imposed except in very special circumstances.

The penalty points system is fairer than the old "totting-up" provisions but it is not uncomplicated and requires explanation. First, it is necessary to understand some preliminary points:

- When points are imposed they are relevant for a period of three years from the date of the *offence* for which they were awarded, not from the date that you appear before the court as used to be the case;

- Generally speaking, a motorist who is convicted of a number of offences which arose out of the same incident, will only have registered on his licence penalty points for one of those offences. For instance, a driver who passes through a red traffic light, is then involved in a collision and upon the arrival of the police is found to be driving with defective brakes, may find himself prosecuted for three offences:

  (a) failing to comply with a traffic light (3 points);
  (b) driving without due care and attention (3-9 points); and
  (c) driving with a vehicle with defective brakes (3 points).

If the points were added together, he would receive a maximum of 15 points, which would make him liable for instant disqualification, and it is worth bearing in mind that Courts do now have the power to "aggregate" points in this way. In the vast majority of cases, however, points will only be awarded for the offence which carries the maximum number. In this case that would be driving without due care and attention, since the maximum for that offence is 9 points, although it may be possible to escape with rather fewer points. This method of imposing points for just one of the offences applies only where the offences were committed on the same occasion. If a motorist is caught speeding four times in one week, he would receive points for each and every offence, making 12 at the least and 24 at the most, since the offences were not committed on the same occasion.

2. VARIABLE POINTS

There are six offences which carry a variable number of penalty points. They are:

- failing to stop after an accident;

- failing to report an accident;
- driving without insurance;
- driving without due care and attention;
- speeding;
- driving otherwise than in accordance with a licence.

In these cases the Court can, in deciding how many points to select, truly reflect its attitude to the gravity of the offence and the offender. Offences committed deliberately, or which illustrate poor driving ability, will incur more points than those committed inadvertently or as a result of minor misjudgement. If you are prosecuted for any of these offences, good mitigation ("mitigation" is explained on page 92) could go a long way towards obtaining the leniency of the Court.

Other offences attract a pre-determined fixed number of points.

3. PENALTY POINTS IN ACTION

When a Court convicts a motorist of a road traffic offence which carries points, it will first consider how many points to award for that particular offence. It will look at the motorist's driving licence to see whether there are any previous points which are significant. Whether disqualification will result is best described by an example:

OFFENCE	DATE COMMITTED	DATE CONVICTED	POINTS
Speeding	12 December 1989	27 January 1990	3
Careless driving	18 August 1990	14 October 1990	4
Defective tyre	3 March 1991	4 May 1991	3

If a driver with the above driving record appears before the Court on 3 February 1993 accused of driving through a red traffic light on 16 October 1992, will he be disqualified? The answer is yes. For the offence now before the Court he will be given 3 points. The Magistrates will then look at his licence and observe that a number of previous offences were committed in the 3 years up to 16

October 1992. There are already 10 points on his licence and a further 3 make 13 which takes him "over the top". It does not matter that a period of more than 3 years has elapsed from the date that he was *convicted* of the first offence, to the date that he now appears before the Court. The relevant period is 3 years from the date that the first offence was *committed*. If the last offence had been committed on 26 December 1992 he would not have been liable to disqualification. In calculating the three year period the Court ignores the actual date of the first and last offence. Therefore the actual period that the motorist is on risk is 3 years and 2 days.

4. THE PERIOD OF DISQUALIFICATION

The usual period of disqualification for totting up 12 points is 6 months. This, however, is the minimum and longer periods can be imposed, although in practice longer periods are fairly unusual. Nevertheless, longer disqualification will be imposed if there has been a previous disqualification for any reason, within 3 years. A minimum of 12 months disqualification will be imposed if there has been one previous disqualification, and a minimum of 2 years will be imposed if there have been 2 or more previous disqualifications. An example may help explain:

OFFENCE	DATE COMMITTED	DATE CONVICTED	PUNISHMENT
Drink/drive	10 October 1989	3 December 1989	Disqualified 1 year
Speeding	4 January 1991	7 March 1991	3 Points
Driving without due care	16 August 1991	27 October 1991	4 Points
Defective brakes	1 November 1991	3 January 1992	3 Points

If a motorist with the above driving record is caught driving without insurance on 15 November 1992 and given a further 6 penalty points, he will be liable to a minimum of

12 months disqualification. The Court will first award him 6 points for driving without insurance, and then see that he has 10 points already on his licence. It will also notice that within the 3 years before the date the insurance offence was committed, he was disqualified for drinking and driving. The Court must now disqualify him for at least 12 months because there has been a previous disqualification. Here it does not matter that more than 3 years have elapsed from the date of the drinking and driving offence being *committed* up to the date that the insurance offence was committed. In calculating *this* 3 year period, it is the date that the disqualification was *imposed* by the Court that is relevant. If in the above example the motorist had been convicted of exceeding the speed limit by more that 30 m.p.h. on 4 January 1991, and was disqualified for 3 months for that offence, there will be two previous relevant disqualifications to take into account, and under the circumstances the Court must now impose a minimum of 2 years disqualification. (To be "relevant" for these purposes, each previous disqualification must have been for a period of not less than 56 days.)

5. ESCAPING DISQUALIFICATION

Even though you might be liable to disqualification under the penalty points system, the Courts may exercise their discretion in your favour under certain limited circumstances and thereby permit you to retain your driving licence. If you can convince a Court that you would suffer "exceptional hardship" then you should not be disqualified.

"Exceptional hardship" is more than mere inconvenience in getting to or from work. If your work *requires* you to drive, you would suffer exceptional hardship if you were disqualified because it would almost certainly lead to the loss of your job. Commercial travellers, bus and lorry drivers are obvious candidates for sympathy. In order to succeed with this plea of mercy, it is necessary for you to attend Court and give evidence on oath. It would be prudent to seek professional advice if you find yourself in this predicament because a few pounds spent on legal help could ensure that you do not lose your job. The excuse of exceptional hardship can, however, only be used once in any period of three years. If you escape disqualification this time, there would be no prospect of saving your licence a second time.

6. ESCAPING POINTS

It is a fact of life that convictions for an endorsable offence will almost certainly result in the imposition of penalty points. There are, however, limited occasions when this will not happen. If it can be proved that there are special reasons which directly relate to the circumstances of the offence, a Magistrates' Court may be prevailed upon to exercise its discretion and to award no endorsement or points. That discretion however is very rarely exercised in a motorist's favour.

In order to succeed, the events that led up to the offence must be exceptional, and the driver must actually give evidence on oath to the Magistrates if he wishes to take advantage of this procedure. Drivers of emergency service vehicles, such as fire engines and ambulances, are prime candidates if they were responding to an emergency call. The ordinary motorist may also be successful in very exceptional circumstances – where, perhaps, a motorist is returning from having a new tyre fitted by a garage, and the wheel falls off the car because the garage did not tighten up the nuts properly, it may be possible to show that this amounts to a "special reason".

Unfortunately a conviction for careless driving will *always* carry penalty points; in deciding to convict, the Court has reached the conclusion that what happened does amount to the offence and in those circumstances the Court has no discretion, but is *bound* to award points.

7. CLEANING UP YOUR LICENCE

Penalty points are only effective for a period of 3 years from the date that the offence was committed. However, it is not possible to have the points, or any endorsement, physically removed from your driving licence until 4 years from the date that they were imposed by the Court; but in the case of points given for drink and driving offences you must wait 11 years. After that period you may apply for a new driving licence. This is done by submitting your existing licence to the Driver and Vehicle Licensing Centre at Swansea, together with an application form and the appropriate fee.

If you are disqualified because you have collected 12 or more points on your licence, then all of your points and endorsements will normally be wiped from your driving licence when it is returned to you. All that will remain on the licence will be details of the disqualification and any relevant previous disqualification. You will start afresh with no penalty points. The only offences that will not disappear in this way are those of dangerous driving; causing death by dangerous driving; and driving offences connected with drink or drugs. The offence of dangerous driving must remain on your licence for 4 years and drink related offences must remain on your licence for 11 years.

If on the other hand you are disqualified not because you have reached the 12 point mark but because of the particular offence you have committed (for example, drink/driving or speeding), then any points which were on the licence before your disqualification will still be there when you get it back (assuming, of course, that they are less than four years old by that time).

If there has been a previous disqualification within 4 years, that will remain on your licence – as will most drinking and driving disqualifications imposed within 11 years.

8. POINTS AND FIXED PENALTIES

Under the fixed penalty procedure, points may be endorsed on your licence without a formal summons to appear before a court. Having surrendered your licence to the police officer who gave you the ticket, your licence will later be returned to you by the Court, with the relevant points marked on it. The procedure is explained in full in Chapter 5, but it is worth noting that a fixed penalty will not be imposed where there is a risk of disqualification, or where you dispute that you actually committed an offence.

Chapter 4

Drinking and driving

The law which regulates drinking and driving was made very much more strict in May 1983. The main purpose was to allow the introduction of new machines for testing and proving a driver's alcohol level, but at the same time a number of ingenious defences which had previously been used were swept away in a package of legislation which now makes it much easier for a drunken driver to be convicted.

1. THE LIMITS

The maximum level of alcohol you may have in your body while driving is 35 microgrammes of alcohol in 100 millilitres of breath. This is equivalent to 80 milligrammes in blood, or 107 milligrammes in urine. Since everyone absorbs alcohol at different rates, it is not realistic to attempt to "translate" the scientific measurements into pints of beer or tots of spirits. Those who drink regularly may feel more capable of driving after drinking than those who drink only occasionally – but if they think they are likely to score less when their sample is analysed they are merely deluding themselves.

Above that scientifically measured limit, you risk prosecution although in practice the police do not normally prosecute unless the breath reading is 40 or more microgrammes. This allows for a certain degree of inaccuracy of measurement. The methods by which alcohol levels are tested are many and varied and not without controversy.

2. ROADSIDE BREATH TESTS

The procedure usually commences with being breathalysed – a roadside breath test, officially known as the "initial" test. This is used as a screening device to separate those who are definitely under the limit from those who may be in excess of it; it is the later testing at the police station that counts if it comes to a prosecution. A police officer in uniform is entitled to require a motorist to undertake this test if he has a "reasonable suspicion" of any of the following:
- that the motorist *is* driving, attempting to drive, or is in charge of a motor vehicle with excess alcohol or while unfit through drink or drugs;
- that the motorist *has been* doing any of those three things and still has alcohol in his body; or
- that the motorist has committed a road traffic offence while in motion.

The officer's "reasonable suspicion" is usually aroused either from the manner in which the vehicle is driven, or, having stopped you for some other legitimate reason, the officer then smells alcohol on your breath. In addition, the police may breathalyse anyone who has been involved in a road accident, even though there is at that stage no suspicion of alcohol.

The officer will ask you to blow into a hand held device and you should follow his instructions carefully. If you have smoked a cigarette within the last 10 minutes or consumed your last drink within the last 20 minutes, you should tell the police officer and it is likely you will have to wait for a short time before taking the test.

If you refuse to take the test, or fail to complete it in the sense that although you have blown into the device, no result has been registered, then you will commit an offence for which the maximum fine is £1,000, and 4 penalty points will be endorsed on your licence. Usually the fine is in the region of 6 units. This offence does not usually result in disqualification by itself unless you are at risk under the penalty points system.

If the test proves positive, or if you fail to provide a result or refuse to take the test, you will be arrested and taken to a police station.

If you have been asked to take a roadside test, but you attempt to escape, the police officer may follow you and may go into your home without a warrant and may arrest you. A police officer has the right to walk up to your front door and he will not be a trespasser unless you happen to have had the forethought to erect large signs denying access to police officers! If the door is opened and the officer asks for the sample but the door is then slammed in his face, he may use force to enter. If he is invited in, and then told to go before he makes his request for a breath sample, he will become a trespasser and any subsequent arrest without a warrant is unlawful. However, even if an unlawful arrest does take place and you are taken to the police station to provide samples of breath, you will not escape conviction solely because the arrest was unlawful in the first place.

Where there has been an accident and there is a suspicion that someone besides the driver has been hurt, the police may go into your home, or any other place where you are believed to be, and if refused entry they may use force. In this instance they will never be trespassers.

It can be very unwise to refuse a police officer's request to provide a sample of breath, even if you claim you were not the driver. One unlucky motorist had his vehicle stolen and it was involved in an accident. The police, who had been given details of the registration number, went to the owner's home. When asked to take a breath test the motorist protested and was arrested. Despite the fact that he claimed he had been at home all the time, he was required to provide two samples of breath into a machine. Again he refused. He was subsequently prosecuted for failing to provide a specimen. At his trial it was indeed proved that he had been at home all along, but he was nevertheless convicted and disqualified from driving. What he should have done was to have complied with the police request, and then established that he had not been the driver at the time in question.

3. BREATH TESTING MACHINES AT THE POLICE STATION

Following an arrest, you will be required to provide two samples of breath into an "evidential breath testing machine" kept at the police station. The best known of these machines is called a Lion Intoximeter although there are others. Certain instructions will be given to you as to how to undertake the test, and these should be carefully followed.

Two samples of breath are required, and the *lower* of the two readings will be relied upon by the police in any proceedings. Where the reading is 50 or less microgrammes (the maximum limit being 35 microgrammes), you have the right, in this borderline case, to insist that a different sort of sample is used in order to determine the amount of alcohol in your body. That different sample will be either blood or urine, although the police may choose which.

If upon arrival at the police station, the breath testing device is not available or is not working, the police officer may insist that you provide a sample of blood or urine, the choice of which being made by the police, and they usually prefer blood! It has been decided that although the breath testing device may at first appear to be working properly, it will be regarded as inoperative if it fails to complete the test. If that happens, then again the police may require blood or urine.

A sample of blood can only be taken with your consent, and must be extracted by a doctor.

If upon your arrival at the police station there appear to be good medical reasons why you should not be required to provide a sample of breath, then the police may elect that you provide a sample of blood or urine. Such occasions may arise where the motorist is asthmatic.

If you are injured in an accident and are admitted to hospital, the police can still require you to provide a sample for analysis. However, the request cannot be made until the doctor in charge of your case has been told of the request and makes no objections. If he does object on the grounds that giving the sample would be prejudicial to your proper care and treatment the police can do nothing further. However, if you are subsequently released by the hospital after initial treatment, there is nothing preventing the police demanding a specimen then.

A motorist who fails to provide a sample of breath, blood or urine, is guilty of an offence which is punishable by a fine of up to £5,000 and you will almost certainly be disqualified. The courts are aware that some motorists, recognising that they are well over the limit, refuse to supply a sample on the basis that if they were to do so they would receive a long period of disqualification. As a consequence, the Courts frequently disqualify for 18 months those who refuse to provide a specimen.

There is a defence to failure to provide a specimen, but proving it is another matter. If you can convince a court that there was a "reasonable excuse" why you did not provide a specimen, then you cannot be convicted. If you are asthmatic you should tell the police officer who will then almost certainly ask for a blood or urine sample instead of a breath sample. If you are a haemophiliac and you are asked to provide blood, you have a good reason for not doing so, but usually a doctor would be asked to confirm your condition. Lastly, there can be few excuses for not providing two samples of urine within an hour or so. So the "reasonable excuse" is inordinately difficult to establish. There was one curious case in which a driver accused of failing to provide a specimen managed to establish that her personal distress at the time amounted to "reasonable excuse", but this does seem quite exceptional.

Before the present stricter law came into effect, you could avoid conviction if you could prove that the police had failed to conform with the procedure to the letter. That no longer applies because a Court will take into account *any* specimen that has been provided, even if the specimen was obtained illegally.

The Court will also assume that the amount of alcohol discovered to be in the specimen represented the amount of alcohol in your body *at the time you were driving,* even though the specimen was taken some short time after you stopped driving. This has largely destroyed the popular "hip flask" defence which was sometimes used by a motorist who had been stopped by the police not while he was actually driving, but later, after he had parked his car. The motorist would then claim that he had had an additional drink after he had finished driving but before the police had breathalysed him, so that the test result did not reflect the alcohol level while he was actually driving. The police would then be unable to establish the alcohol level at the time of driving.

Under the present legislation, the tables are turned and a motorist who wishes to raise this defence would have to prove that *if he had not consumed that additional drink* he would have been *under* the limit. In practice this is very difficult. It would be necessary to rely on complex medical evidence to confirm the amount of alcohol in your body at the time, the rate at which your body broke down that alcohol, the amount of alcohol that you had consumed before driving and the amount of alcohol you consumed after you had finished driving. Thus the task of proving this complex matter has now been thrown squarely back onto the motorist himself.

4. DRIVING OR ATTEMPTING TO DRIVE WITH EXCESS ALCOHOL

You may not drive or attempt to drive when over the alcohol limit set out at the beginning of this Chapter. Although you would of course be stationary when the police officer challenges you with driving while above the limit, it will nevertheless be accepted that you were driving. In "attempting" to drive it does not matter that it would not in fact have been possible to drive because of damage to your vehicle or some injury to you. It is the *attempt* which is all important.

The maximum penalty is £5,000 fine and/or six months' imprisonment and disqualification. In practice you are likely to be fined at least 20 units and disqualified.

5. DRIVING OR ATTEMPTING TO DRIVE WHEN UNFIT THROUGH DRINK OR DRUGS

Prosecutions for these offences are now far less common than they used to be. "Driving" and "attempting" have the same meanings as explained in the paragraph above. Whether you are unfit is a question of fact, usually determined by some medical evidence. The prosecution would not have to prove that you were so incapable that you would not have been able to drive a car.

6. IN CHARGE OF A MOTOR VEHICLE WITH EXCESS ALCOHOL OR WHILE UNFIT

The term "in charge" has caused a great deal of legal argument. If you are caught "sleeping it off" in your car, you may still be "in charge". Likewise if you are stopped on your way to your car, in possession of the keys, you will be "in charge". Indeed the motorist who, having been involved in an accident, ran off and was subsequently caught half a mile away was still said to be "in charge". There is one possible escape route – if you can prove to the satisfaction of the Court that there was no prospect of your driving while over the limit you cannot be convicted.

The penalty for these offences is a maximum fine of £2,500 and/or three months in prison. In practice the likely fine is around 12 units.

7. REFUSAL TO PROVIDE A SPECIMEN

It is an offence to refuse a roadside breath test. It is also a separate offence to refuse to provide a specimen for analysis at the police station. There are separate punishments for each offence.

If you refuse or fail to provide a specimen for a roadside breath test the maximum fine is £1,000, although in practice something in the region of 6 units is likely. In addition 4 penalty points will be imposed. It follows that you will not be disqualified for this offence unless the penalty points bring your total to 12.

As explained earlier in this Chapter, it is also an offence to refuse to provide a specimen for analysis at the police station. For this offence disqualification is almost certain. If you are convicted of driving *or attempting to drive* and then refusing to provide a specimen, then unless you can prove "reasonable excuse" (explained on page 61), you will be disqualified for at least 18 months. If, however, the conviction is for being *in charge* and then failing to provide a specimen you might not be disqualified but instead receive 10 penalty points.

The financial punishments for failing to provide a specimen for analysis also depend on whether you were driving or attempting to drive, or in charge. In the first case, the maximum fine is £5,000, and around 24 units can be expected; in the second case, the maximum is £2,500 with 12 units being likely.

8. DISQUALIFICATION FOR DRINK/DRIVING OFFENCES

With the exception of the "in charge" offences, a conviction for a drink and driving offence brings with it *automatic* disqualification. You will be disqualified from driving for at least 12 months, but it can be longer depending on how much you were over the limit. The table below shows the periods of disqualification usually imposed for a first offender:

Period of disqualification	Amount of alcohol in your body exceeding the figures below in 100 millilitre samples		
	BREATH (microgrammes)	BLOOD (milligrammes)	URINE (milligrammes)
12 months	35	80	107
18 months	66	150	200
2 years	88	200	267
3 years	110	250	333

If you are convicted again for a second, or further, drinking and driving offence within 10 years of your first, you will be disqualified for not less than 3 years.

Disqualification is not *automatic* for an offence of being "in charge" of a motor vehicle with excess alcohol, or whilst unfit, but it is frequently the consequence nevertheless.

Whilst it is true to say that the Court is *obliged* to disqualify you for the other drinking and driving offences, there are very limited situations where this can be avoided, but it is an extremely difficult matter. If you can show that, without your knowledge, your drinks had been "laced" and, furthermore, it was that additional alcohol which brought you over the limit, you may stand a small chance of avoiding disqualification. However, the discretion of the court is only likely to be exercised in your favour where there is reliable and substantial evidence that this is the case and where the level of intoxication was not high.

Another limited means of avoiding disqualification is to prove to the Court that you were responding to an emergency. However, the emergency must be real and not fanciful. You must have considered every other possible means of getting to where you are required to go without having to drive. The emergency must be something that could not have been anticipated. An expectant father who finds himself rushing his wife to hospital will not avoid a disqualification – because the emergency could have been anticipated. In reality, disqualification will be imposed for drinking and driving offences and it is only in the rarest of cases where the Magistrates will exercise their discretion not to.

When dealing with an accusation that you refused to provide a specimen for analysis, the Courts are well aware that many motorists refuse because they know they are over the limit and if tested will probably be disqualified for more than the minimum 12 months. For this reason, the Courts are highly likely to disqualify for 18 months if it is proved that you failed to provide a specimen.

If you commit two separate drinking and driving offences within 10 years of each other, there is no guarantee your driving licence will be returned to you when your period of disqualification comes to an end.

Your licence will also not be returned to you as a matter of course where:

- you were disqualified by a court for being at least 2.5 times over the legal limit; or
- you were disqualified for refusing to provide a specimen for analysis.

In these circumstances you will be notified by the Driver and Vehicle Licensing Centre at Swansea and required to submit to a special medical examination in order to determine whether you have a drink problem.

9. CAUSING DEATH BY CARELESS DRIVING WHEN UNDER THE INFLUENCE OF DRINK OR DRUGS

This new and very serious offence was introduced in July 1992 in response to public concern at the often appalling consequences of the actions of those who drive carelessly while under the influence of intoxicants. It is committed by someone who causes the death of another person by driving carelessly or without reasonable consideration (see page 34) and who either:

- is unfit to drive through drink or drugs (see page 63); or
- is over the legal alcohol limit (see page 57); or
- fails to provide a specimen for analysis (see page 64).

This is a matter which can only be dealt with by the Crown Court and for which the services of a solicitor are essential. The maximum penalty is 5 years' imprisonment and there is also a compulsory disqualification period of not less than 2 years.

Chapter 5

Fixed penalties

1. THE SYSTEM

Although in this country we do not have a system of "on the spot" fines, parking offences have for many years been dealt with by means of a fixed penalty – the "parking ticket". This requires you to pay a fine within a given period and if you do not pay you risk being prosecuted.

In 1986 the fixed penalty system was vastly extended to allow many more offences, including endorsable ones, to become subject to fixed penalties. The object of the exercise was to relieve the Courts of some of their heavy burden and to encourage motorists to pay quickly for their mistakes. Throughout the other Chapters of this book there are references to the offences which can be dealt with in this way; they include:

- speeding;
- failure to comply with traffic lights or traffic signs;
- driving a vehicle with defective brakes, steering or tyres or any other matter which is a breach of the "Construction and Use" Regulations mentioned on page 26;
- leaving your vehicle in a dangerous position;
- driving without the appropriate licence or in breach of the restrictions applying to provisional licence holders;
- certain pedestrian crossing offences;

- failure to display your tax disc; and
- a number of other minor and less common offences.

In many cases, motorists of average means will be happy to pay a fixed penalty since it will often cost far less than the unit fine which would result from being prosecuted and convicted. As can be seen from a glance at the Table on page 119, there are very few cases where the "usual" unit fine is likely to amount to as little as the £20 or £40 fixed penalty. At first sight, people of very limited means might think that a unit fine based upon a disposable weekly income of perhaps as little as the minimum £4 would be a better bet; but appearances, alas, can be deceptive. In these circumstances the law allows the Courts to put the unit fine system to one side and increase the fine for a "fixed penalty" offence to the level of the appropriate fixed penalty! Another bonus in favour of accepting a fixed penalty if you have committed a speeding or driving licence offence is that the penalty points which will be endorsed on your licence will be fixed at 3, whereas if you go to Court you could receive any number between 3 and 6. It should be noted, however, that the amount of fixed penalties can be increased from time to time by the Government. In addition, in serious cases, for example where the speed limit has been exceeded by more than 30 m.p.h., the police may decide to prosecute in the usual way rather than give a fixed penalty.

It is worth mentioning too that there are special provisions to protect car hire companies from having to pay out large sums of money in fixed penalties on behalf of their customers!

In the first place, it is important to distinguish between those offences which carry penalty points and those which do not, since the procedure differs accordingly. If the offence is one for which penalty points *can* be imposed, the "fixed penalty notice" (explained below) must be given to the driver personally by a police officer in uniform. In the case of an offence which does not attract points, the notice may be left on the vehicle by either a police officer or a traffic warden.

2. OFFENCES WHICH DO NOT CARRY PENALTY POINTS

A police officer in uniform or a traffic warden who suspects that you have committed a fixed penalty offence which does not carry penalty points may issue you with a "fixed penalty notice" – a ticket. It may be given to you personally or placed under your windscreen wiper. The notice gives details about the offence; tells you the amount of the penalty (£20), and that it must be paid within 28 days; and gives the address of the Magistrates' Court for the area where the offence was committed and to which the money must be sent. The notice also tells you that if you dispute that an offence was committed you may, again within 28 days, ask that the matter be decided by a Court, and explains the procedure for doing so.

If you pay the penalty within 28 days, that is the end of the matter and you cannot be prosecuted for the offence. If you do not pay and do not ask for a Court hearing within the 28 days, the next step will depend on whether you were given the fixed penalty notice in person or it was fixed to your vehicle.

If it was handed to you, then a fine equivalent to the amount of the fixed penalty plus a further 50% (making £30) will be registered against you at the Magistrates' Court. This is obviously intended to encourage you to pay promptly. Once the fine had been registered the Court can take steps to make sure you pay it – including issuing a warrant for your arrest if necessary. If you do not live in the area where the offence was committed, the Court covering the area where you do live will carry out this enforcement procedure.

Where the notice was simply left on the vehicle, the police may send a separate "notice to owner" to the person whose name appears as the registered owner on the

Vehicle Registration Document. This fresh notice will inform the owner that a fixed penalty notice was issued and the circumstances in which it was done. It will require the fixed penalty to be paid within 28 days unless the owner either requests a Court hearing or completes a "statutory statement of ownership", or a "statutory statement of ownership" *and* a "statutory statement of facts".

You would complete the "statutory statement of ownership" if, for example, you had sold your vehicle before the offence was committed but the new ownership had not been recorded at Swansea. In this document you will state either that you have never owned the vehicle, or that you had sold it, in which case you should give details of the person to whom you sold it if you are able.

If the vehicle was indeed yours but you were not driving it at the time in question, then you should complete the "statutory statement of ownership" in which you will confirm you are the owner, *and* a "statutory statement of facts" stating who was the driver at the time. If the person who was driving also signs the "statutory statement of facts", then the driver is in effect disputing the offence and asking for a Court hearing, unless of course he decides to pay the fixed penalty.

If you do not complete either of these two documents and do not ask for a Court hearing, you, the owner, must pay the fixed penalty. If you do so, you will hear no more. If you do not do so, a fine can be registered against you in the Magistrates' Court of the amount of the fixed penalty plus 50%, and enforced as explained above.

In an effort to discourage those who might be tempted to complete the forms with false information, a fine of up to £5,000 may be imposed if it transpires that you did so.

3. OFFENCES WHICH DO CARRY PENALTY POINTS

Where the offence does attract penalty points, things are rather different. In such a case a fixed penalty notice may only be issued by a police officer in uniform (not a traffic warden) and certain requirements must be fulfilled. In these cases the fixed penalty notice must be given personally, it cannot be left on the vehicle.

Having informed you that a fixed penalty offence has been committed the police officer will ask you for your driving licence. If you have it with you, he will look at it to see if you would be liable to disqualification under the penalty points system if convicted of this offence. Provided that you would not, he will ask to retain your driving licence and if you agree he will issue you with a fixed penalty notice. As above, this specifies the nature of the offence, the amount of the penalty (£40 for an offence carrying points); when and where it is to be paid; and that you may request a Court hearing if you dispute that an offence was committed.

You will be given a receipt for your driving licence which will be valid for two months. Further receipts can be obtained from the Court. Until your driving licence is returned to you, these receipts can be used in place of the licence itself if, for example, you are asked to produce your documents to a police station. If you neither pay nor request a court hearing within 28 days, a fine equivalent to the amount of the fixed penalty plus a further 50% (making £60) will be registered against you and may be enforced in the usual way. Your driving licence must, however, be returned to you once the points have been endorsed upon it. If you pay the fixed penalty within 28 days, that will be the end of the matter and your licence will be returned to you once the points have been endorsed on it.

If you do not have your driving licence with you when you are pulled up for a fixed penalty offence, the police officer will issue you with a "provisional fixed penalty notice" and you are required to produce this, together with your driving licence, within 7 days, to a police station of your choice. Provided that you are not liable to disqualification and agree to leave your driving licence at the police station, a normal fixed penalty notice will then be handed to you.

If your driving licence shows that a conviction for the present offence would bring your penalty points to 12 or more and render you liable to disqualification, regardless of whether you produce your licence at the time or later at a police station, then the fixed penalty procedure cannot be used and instead you will be reported for prosecution in the normal way. If you refuse to allow the police to retain your driving licence, whether produced at the time or later, the fixed penalty procedure cannot be adopted. It is wise to think carefully before refusing to let your driving licence be kept by the police – the fixed penalty will often be far less than the fine you might get if prosecuted and convicted.

4. THE AMOUNT

The amount of a fixed penalty is as follows:
- £40 for an offence which carries penalty points;
- £40 for illegal parking on a 'Red Route' in London;
- £30 for illegal parking elsewhere in London; and
- £20 for illegal parking outside London and for all other non-endorsable offences.

A 50% surcharge will be added to these figures if you do not respond to a fixed penalty notice and a fine is registered against you, and you will then have to pay £60, £45 or £30 as appropriate. These are the amounts presently being levied, but it is of course possible that they may be increased from time to time in the future.

5. A NEW SYSTEM FOR THE FUTURE

As a result of a change in the law in July 1992, police forces are now able to install camera equipment in various places for the automatic detection of speeding and traffic light offences. Since no police officer will be present to hand a fixed penalty notice to the driver on the spot, a different system has been devised for dealing with these offences. It is called the "conditional offer" system, and under it the police may send a notice offering a fixed penalty (the "conditional offer") to the supposed offender through the post. The notice will give him 28 days in which to send both his licence and the requisite payment to the appropriate place; provided that he does so and that the points to be added for the offence in question will not bring the total on the licence to 12 or more, it will be endorsed and returned to its owner in the usual way.

6. REQUESTING A COURT HEARING

Whether or not penalty points are awardable, if you have received a fixed penalty notice and dispute that an offence has been committed, you have the right to insist that the question should be determined by the Court. You must, however, give notice of your intention within 28 days. Having given the requisite notice, you will be advised in due course of the date that you are to appear before the Court. If you are convicted then the fine which is imposed upon you may well exceed the amount of the fixed penalty. You are also likely to be required to pay the prosecution's costs. It follows, therefore, that you should think carefully before deciding to contest an allegation.

Chapter 6

Going to court

Given today's road traffic conditions and the complex legislation which controls our behaviour on the road, you will be doing extremely well to complete your driving career without ever being prosecuted for an offence. If you are unlucky enough to have a summons dropped through your letterbox you will need to consider carefully and decide what to do about it.

1. THE SUMMONS

A summons is a document issued by a Court requiring your attendance before the Court on a specified date in order to answer an allegation which has been made against you, usually by the police. The summons tells you of the offence you are said to have committed, although it need not go into detail.

In normal circumstances, you must attend court personally in response to the summons, but if you do not, a warrant for your arrest may only be issued if:

- it can be proved that the summons was served upon you *and*
- either –
  - (a) the offence is one where imprisonment may be imposed or,
  - (b) having convicted you in your absence, the Court is

considering disqualification.

However, there is one very important exception to the above. The vast majority of motoring summonses allow the offender to plead Guilty by post if he or she so chooses. If this applies, then the summons and the accompanying papers will explain what has to be done. In such cases you can also obtain more time to prepare yourself by writing to the Court asking for an adjournment. If you intend to plead Not Guilty then provided you tell the Court in writing, you need not attend on the date shown in the summons, since on this occasion the Court will simply be granting the adjournment.

In many, though not all, cases, the summons will have attached to it a "statement of facts". This does not form part of the summons and if it contains an error, that does not invalidate the proceedings. The purpose of the statement of facts is two-fold. First, should you elect to plead Guilty by post only that statement will be read to the Court by the prosecution; and secondly it gives you an idea about the nature of the complaint which is being made about your driving. If your summons does not contain a statement of facts it is worthwhile writing to the police with a request for information.

2. THE COURT

With the exception of causing death by dangerous driving, or by careless driving when under the influence of drink or drugs, almost all offences are dealt with in a Magistrates' Court. The Courts are scattered throughout the country and are frequently found near police stations. They vary in size, shape and architectural quality. The Court usually comprises 2 or 3 magistrates who come from all walks of life and generally do not have legal qualifications. Occasionally the court may consist of one "Stipendiary Magistrate" who is legally qualified.

The task of the Magistrates is to listen to and assess the evidence and then come to a conclusion about the facts of the case. They are assisted by a legal adviser, who is legally trained, and who sits at a desk in front of them. He or she will deal with the preliminary matters such as confirming your name, address and date of birth, and will put the allegation to you. The most important function of the legal adviser is to advise the Magistrates on any points of law which may arise in the course of a case. When addressing the Magistrates it is usual to refer to them as "Your Worship", "Sir" or "Madam".

You may well not be familiar with the atmosphere in Court. It is not as difficult as sometimes made out on television, but it is serious and the Court should be treated with respect. You should remember that the Magistrates are ordinary human beings who are interested in finding out what actually happened and they will usually apply common sense when assessing whether or not you are guilty. It is also worth bearing in mind that the majority of road traffic cases are about the facts – establishing what actually happened – rather than complicated points of law.

3. SOLICITORS

If you accept what is said about your driving and intend to plead Guilty you may take the view that the additional expense involved in employing a solicitor will not make any great difference to the amount of fine you will have to pay at the end. In that case you may decide to write a letter "in mitigation" to try and escape with as small a punishment as possible. Chapter 7 sets out many sample letters of this kind and should help in composing a suitable explanation.

If, on the other hand, you are accused of a serious offence, or you dispute what is said against you, then it may be time for a contest. If the case is contested, the prosecution will be conducted by a representative of the Crown Prosecution Service, who will be either a solicitor or a barrister. This means that in many ways it would be better if you too have the assistance of a professional. However, the cost of employing a solicitor may be prohibitive and in the circumstances you may decide to deal with the matter yourself.

Regrettably, financial assistance from the State for legal proceedings (legal aid) is not normally available to motorists, except in extremely serious cases such as causing death by dangerous driving. But if you have been involved in an accident, your insurance company may be prepared to pay for you to have a solicitor if you are prosecuted following the accident. If you are a member of a trade union the union may provide some free legal advice through their own solicitors.

If neither of these facilities is available, it might well be wise to spend a few pounds obtaining some preliminary legal advice. A solicitor should be able to find out from the police the nature of their evidence, and then advise you on your prospects of success in fighting them. If you have no chance of winning, there is no point in fighting, for you will probably have to pay the prosecution's costs and witnesses's expenses as well as the fine.

It is often difficult to be dispassionate about a motoring offence in which you are involved, but the decision of a Court will be based upon the facts put before it. If that evidence is overwhelming, and the prospects of being found Not Guilty are negligible, it may be economical to swallow your pride and plead Guilty.

4. GUILTY OR NOT GUILTY?

When you receive a summons, it will show the date you are to appear at Court and the matter will be dealt with on that day if you plead Guilty. But if you have not decided whether to plead Guilty or Not Guilty and need time to obtain preliminary legal advice or to make inquiries you should write a letter to the Court asking for an "adjournment" – ie for the matter to be postponed. Until you have decided which way to plead, you should not give the

Court any indication of what you intend.

But once you do decide to plead Not Guilty, you should write to the Court telling them so. The papers will then be sent to the prosecuting solicitors, who will be present at Court when the case is dealt with. If, having started by pleading Not Guilty, you later change your mind and plead Guilty, you may be faced with paying the prosecution's costs which could otherwise have been avoided.

If you are firmly resolved to plead Not Guilty to the offence, then you will be notified by the Court of the date that the matter is fixed for hearing. You must then set about preparing yourself. Although you may not be able to afford a solicitor, or prefer not to employ one, you may manage to avoid being convicted if you are well prepared and can turn the evidence in your favour.

5. PREPARING YOUR OWN DEFENCE

To most motorists, an appearance in Court is an unfamiliar and probably unnerving experience. However, at the hearing the Court will usually be prepared to assist you all they can in presenting your case properly, and you should accept their help for the Court will not be impressed if you appear deliberately difficult or obstructive. Ultimately the burden rests on you – and you should be well prepared.

Precisely what steps you should take will depend on exactly what is said against you. If there was a witness, or witnesses, to the incident in question, you should see him or her and get them to write down and sign their version of the events; or write it for them and ask them to check and sign it – this document then becomes their "statement". If those statements are helpful to you, you should ask the witness or witnesses to come to Court on the day fixed for the hearing. If they are reluctant to do so, you can request the Court to issue a "witness summons" which obliges them to attend.

The procedure for obtaining a witness summons varies

from court to court. Some courts require you to attend in person, while others will accept a written request. You should telephone the court to find out what they want you to do. Whether you go in person or write, you must give the name and address of the witness and tell the Court that he or she is reluctant to attend voluntarily. You should ask the Court to serve the witness summons, which they usually do by post. You should start this procedure as soon as you know the date of the hearing rather than leave it till later and risk that there may not be enough time to serve the summons.

If photographs or a sketch plan would help the Court to understand your version of the matter, you may prepare these yourself, or, if someone else does it for you, you should make certain that that person will be at Court to confirm them if necessary.

You should consider carefully the allegation against you and work out how the witnesses can help you, writing down in advance the questions you will wish to ask them at the hearing. Bear in mind that at the hearing itself, the rules of evidence say that neither you nor the witness will be allowed to look at the statements written earlier. The section at the end of this Chapter will give help in deciding what questions you may need to ask and what points may need clarifying.

At some time before the hearing the police may send to you the statement of one or more of their witnesses to see if you agree with what they have to say, so as to clarify the areas of dispute. Normally the statements sent in this way are uncontroversial. Accompanying them will be a form to complete requesting you to indicate whether or not you agree the statement. Read the statement(s) carefully; if, and only if, there is something significant with which you disagree, should you dispute the statement and mark the form that you require the witness to attend at the Court to give evidence. If you require the witness or witnesses to attend and you are subsequently convicted you may well be required to pay their expenses for attending court. However if there is something with which you strongly disagree, you should not hesitate to inform the police that you require the witness's attendance at Court. If you do not respond to the notice it will be presumed that you do not dispute the statement and that it can be read out to the Court at the trial.

6. THE HEARING

On the day of the hearing you should arrive well in time. You should notify the usher of your attendance and in due course the Court will be ready for you. You will stand before the Magistrates and will be asked to confirm your name, address and probably your date of birth. The allegation will be read to you and you will formally plead Not Guilty. It may be appropriate at this stage to ask the Court if you could sit at a desk, as you may wish to take notes of anything said by the witnesses (you should of course come armed with a pen and paper). The Court ought to agree to this request, but it is a matter for the Magistrates.

The prosecuting solicitor will then outline his case to the Magistrates and begin by calling his witnesses, who may indeed include the police officer or officers who were involved following the incident in question. He will ask them a number of questions. You should make a note of anything said by a witness with which you disagree. You will then be able to question ("cross examine") that witness. You should ask the witness questions on matters about which he may have something to say which bears on the points you intend to raise in your defence; you should also challenge anything he has said with which you disagree. When you have finished with the witness, the prosecuting solicitor may ask them some supplementary questions. This procedure is adopted with each witness until the prosecution have finished their case. It is then your opportunity to give evidence.

First, you will give your own version of the facts, and you should tell the Court as concisely as possible your account of the matter. You should introduce everything you feel to be relevant. When you have finished, you will be cross examined by the prosecuting solicitor. There are a number of points that you need to consider when answering his questions. If you do not hear a question, do not be frightened to ask that it be repeated. If you are asked a question and cannot understand what is being requested, you should not be hesitant about requesting that the matter be put in a different way. You should not be led into the realms of speculation. You can give evidence only about what you saw and what you did. You should take your evidence at your own speed. The Magistrates will have heard the question and will be interested in the answer. You should think carefully before answering any question and you should keep your answers as short as possible.

After cross examination you have the opportunity of speaking again to clarify anything that has arisen while you were being questioned by the prosecution. When your own evidence has been completed you are entitled to call upon your witnesses. Each witness will be dealt with in the same way as the prosecution witnesses, although this time you will begin the questioning. If you are wise you will have obtained a statement before the hearing and worked out from it what questions to ask. Each witness will be cross examined by the prosecution when you have finished your questions, and you will finally have the opportunity of clarifying any points that have arisen out of their cross examination. When all the evidence has been presented you will be able to sum it all up to the Magistrates and indicate to them why, in your opinion, you should be found Not Guilty.

The Court will then consider everything they have heard and determine whether or not you are Guilty. In order to be found Guilty, the prosecution must have proved their case "beyond reasonable doubt" and if there is doubt, it should be resolved in your favour. If you have prepared yourself in a logical and careful manner the chances of convincing the Court of your innocence are the greater.

The Magistrates may retire to consider their verdict, and then return to Court to announce the decision. Or they may reach their decision and announce it without leaving the Court.

If you are unfortunate enough to fail, and are found Guilty, the Court will then consider how to punish you – a matter upon which much is said elsewhere in this book. It is usual to impose a unit fine, the number of units depending principally on the seriousness of the offence (please see page 15 for a description of the unit fine system). You will be asked to fill in a simple "means enquiry" form so that the Court can properly assess the value of each unit in your case. The form will tell you that if you don't complete it, the Court may decide that you can pay a fine based on a spare weekly income of up to £100 a week, so it is in most people's interests to supply the relevant information! In any event, failure to comply is itself an offence, as is attempting to deceive the Court. Once it has been fixed, the Court will expect the fine to be paid quickly since it is intended to be a punishment, not a mere inconvenience. If you cannot pay there and then you may ask for time to pay – eg 28 days to pay the whole amount, or to pay a certain amount per week. If you ask to pay by instalments, you will be invited to make an offer as to the amount per week, but if it is not acceptable the Court will decide how much you pay off each week.

If the offence for which you have been convicted carries penalty points your driving licence will be retained by the Court so that the relevant details can be recorded upon it and the Driving and Vehicle Licensing Centre at Swansea will be notified. If for some reason you are disqualified you will be told of the consequences should you drive during that period, including the risk of imprisonment.

7. SOME EXAMPLES

Skilful cross examination is an art achieved after many

years of experience. The questions you will need to ask of the witnesses at the hearing vary depending upon the nature of the allegation. By way of guidance the rest of this Chapter is devoted to hints on how to tackle the most common motoring offences. Dangerous driving and drink related offences are not included. These are either extremely complicated or so serious that it would be fool-hardy to try and deal with the matter yourself.

While you may feel that a witness is distorting the truth it is counter-productive simply to contradict him or her, especially if he or she is an independent witness with no axe to grind and no personal interest in the matter. It is far better to suggest that the witness is mistaken and point out to them why you believe they have got it wrong.

Cross examining police officers can be very difficult. Invariably they will seek the Court's permission to refer to their pocket book, and provided the notes were made at the time of or shortly after the incident in question, it is extraordinarily difficult to take objection. If any significant interval elapsed between the time of, say, a conversation and its being recorded in the police notebook, you could put the officer to the test by asking him to repeat the last few questions which have been asked in Court and the answers. However, make sure you have written them down carefully yourself so that you may check how good his memory really is.

No Driving Licence

If you drive a motor vehicle when you have no licence or you are not entitled to drive that sort of vehicle there is no excuse and therefore no point attempting to defend such a case. You may however be prosecuted for driving without a licence as an alternative to failing to produce your driving licence to the police when required to do so, as outlined on pages 41-42. If this happens, and you are then able to produce your licence to the Court, the more serious offence of driving without a licence will be withdrawn but you will still be prosecuted for failing to produce.

A contest could take place where it is alleged that you permitted or "aided and abetted" someone else to drive without a licence. Here it is a question of what was in your mind and whether you had taken reasonable steps to ensure that no offence was committed. In practical terms there is unlikely to be much to dispute in the prosecution's case. The police will say that having stopped the driver for some reason it was discovered that he or she held no driving licence and, perhaps, that it was your vehicle which you had loaned to the driver. The police officers may relate to the Court a conversation which they had with you and if there is to be any dispute it will be here. If they say you told them that the driver did not have a licence or you confessed to having asked no questions before lending the vehicle, then you may disagree. You should then put it to the officer that he is mistaken. You would then, if appropriate, give evidence that you had asked and been told that the driver had a licence. It would also be wise to have the driver at Court as your witness to confirm this. If the driver is reluctant to come to Court you may compel him to do so by asking the Court to issue a witness summons as explained on page 79.

No Insurance

Once again, the production of an insurance certificate relevant for the period in question is likely to result in the prosecution withdrawing a summons. If the case arose because you did not produce your insurance certificate when required to do so by the police, but you do produce it to the Court, the Court will proceed only on the lesser allegation of failure to produce. However, the certificate of insurance must actually have entitled you to drive. Insurance policies are either restricted to the owner, named drivers, or anyone with the owner's permission. If you were driving a vehicle with permission, it would be wise to have the owner at Court to confirm this.

With one exception, there is no defence to driving without insurance. Neither is there any defence to permitting someone else to do so. These are "absolute" offences – if there is no insurance you will be convicted no matter how careful you were. If you allowed someone else to drive your car and there was no insurance covering them, you will still be guilty of an offence even if you genuinely but mistakenly believed they were insured to drive. In these circumstances all that is left is mitigation – dealt with in the next Chapter – in the hope that the Court will be lenient.

You will however have a defence if you were driving your employer's vehicle in the honest belief that you were insured. You would have to prove to the Court that it was your employer's obligation to insure you to drive and it would be wise to bring him to Court or at least have a letter confirming that the lack of insurance was his mistake. In such cases the prosecution's evidence is likely to be beyond dispute and need not be challenged. You will simply rely on your own evidence and that of your employer.

MOT and Tax Disc
The only defence you may have to an allegation of using a vehicle without an MOT Certificate or a tax disc is to be able to prove that you were on your way directly to or from the nearest convenient MOT testing station, as explained on pages 25–26. You could cross examine a police officer as to whether or not you told him that was the case and if necessary you should call someone from the garage to confirm that your car had in fact been booked in for an MOT. Obviously, in the case of the absence of the tax disc this defence will only work if the car is three or more years old and therefore needs to have an MOT.

If your tax disc was not properly displayed there is no defence, even if it fell from the windscreen while your vehicle was parked.

Roadworthy Condition
If you are accused of having defective brakes, steering or tyres, or if your vehicle is said to be in a dangerous condi-

tion, it is a matter of establishing the nature and extent of the defect. If you disagree with what the police officer had to say at the time, then hopefully you will have had your vehicle inspected by a garage immediatcly afterwards. If the garage confirmed that your vehicle was roadworthy, you should arrange for a representative of the garage to be at Court to give evidence in your favour. You will have to question the police officer carefully about what he says he found. Things might get technical and to a large extent you will have to rely on what the garage told you. You can suggest to the police officer that he was mistaken but in most cases your defence will succeed or fail on the garage evidence.

Speeding

It is very difficult to avoid a conviction for speeding, especially if you were caught in a radar speed trap or by Vascar. You should remember that if you have exceeded the speed limit by *any* amount, be it as little as half an m.p.h., then you are guilty of an offence, and should plead guilty, even though you may take issue with the alleged speed. But if you are convinced you were not exceeding the limit, and plead not guilty, you could cross examine the police officers as to whether there were any other vehicles that might have caused them to misjudge your speed, and if there was anyone in your car with you, then you could rely upon their evidence to confirm your actual speedometer reading at the time.

If your speed was determined by the use of a hand held radar gun, then you should question the police officer as to its use. If there are any large road signs, or radio stations close by, or other obstacles that could have caused the beam to be deflected, photographs of that area would be helpful, and you can then put your allegation to the police officer. If you were followed by a police vehicle it may be relevant as to how far they remained behind you when checking your speed and for how long.

Pedestrian Crossings, Traffic Lights and Road Signs

Defending these cases is largely a matter of casting doubt on what the police say they saw. If your vehicle reaches the black and white markings before the pedestrian put his foot on a crossing, then no offence has been committed. Similarly, if you have crossed the stop line of the set of traffic lights while they were showing amber, you should not be convicted. If the police officer was a substantial distance away from the crossing, stop line, or whatever it may be, you could put it to him that he was mistaken, and back this up by any witnesses who may have been in your vehicle. Similarly, allegations of a failure to obey road signs or white lines on the road will depend upon what was seen, by whom, and how far away they were.

Careless Driving

What does and does not amount to careless driving is a question of the facts and will be determined by the Court on the basis of the evidence presented to it. It is probably the most contested of all motoring offences. There could be any number of witnesses, each of whom may give a different account of what happened.

You will have your own view as to what happened, and it is not necessarily easy to convince the witness to accept your point of view. It is important therefore that the witnesses are closely questioned, especially if they say something that you do not agree with. Anything that you wish to raise in your defence must be put to the witnesses. How far away they were from the incident, and what they were doing at the time it took place are important to the Court in assessing the accuracy of what they say and these matters should be brought out from the questioning. It is essential to make a note of precisely what the witnesses say, so that when you make your submission to the Magistrates you will be able to highlight the differences in your favour.

Precisely what questions you will have to ask will depend entirely upon the circumstances of the event. For example, if it is said that you drove out of a minor road and were subsequently involved in a collision with a vehicle on the main road, it could be important to establish that the other vehicle was being driven at a substantial speed and that when you began your manoeuvre it was not in sight. If it is alleged that you ran into the back of someone else, it may be a question of establishing that in fact they reversed into you, or perhaps braked severely for no apparent reason.

Failure to Produce Documents

Failure to produce driving documents will usually be determined by paperwork and supporting evidence. The police officer issuing HORT 1 (see page 41) may be called to confirm the HORT 1 which he gave you. That is likely to be beyond challenge. The police officer at the police station where the documents should have been produced may also confirm that having consulted the records, no documents were produced, or the document in question was not produced. If there is any dispute it is likely to be here. You would have to cross examine the police officer who no doubt would produce HORT 2 (which is the paperwork completed at the police station when you produce your documents), which ought to indicate whether the document(s) in question have been produced. In reality, you are likely to make little headway unless you can prove there was an error in the paperwork – by no means easy in most circumstances.

However, there is now a new line of defence – if you can show it was not reasonably practicable to produce the document(s) before the date on which the police decide to prosecute. If, for example, your licence was at Swansea to have a change of address recorded you may escape conviction.

Dangerous Parking and Obstruction

If it is alleged that you parked your vehicle in a dangerous position, then again it is a question of establishing the exact facts so that the Court may decide whether or not they amount to the offence charged. You could attempt to cast doubt on the evidence of those who say you parked within the zig-zags of a zebra-crossing, on a blind bend or on the brow of a hill. Photographs may be important. You can then get the various witnesses to show precisely where they say your vehicle was parked.

If it is said you obstructed the highway, again there may be a dispute as to the facts, or you may avoid conviction if you can show that your vehicle had broken down.

Motorway Offences

If you are charged with an offence that can only arise on the motorway, it is a matter of challenging the evidence of anyone who says that you committed an offence. Little headway is likely to be made in respect of allegations of reversing on the carriageway, driving in the wrong direction, making a "U" turn or driving on the hard shoulder if those actions were observed by police officers.

However, if it is said that you stopped your vehicle on the hard shoulder then you have an excuse if you can show that your vehicle had broken down, or had run out of petrol, oil or water which it required in order to be used. You may be able to show you sought help and the garage or motorists service who came to your aid may be able to confirm what happened.

If it is said that you towed a trailer in the third lane of a motorway, that again is a question of evidence and witnesses would have to be challenged as to precisely what they saw and, if appropriate, as to whether or not there was a wide load occupying the other two lanes.

Lighting your Vehicle

Eye witness evidence is essential before it can be shown that an offence has been committed but you may be able to convince the Court that you had taken all reasonable precautions to ensure that your lights were working properly. It is easier to show that you were unaware a back light was not working rather than a front light which ought to be apparent from driving.

Seat Belts

Allegations that you were not wearing a seat belt are sometimes made but a prosecution is only likely to take place when this has been observed by a police officer. If the alleged offence occurs during darkness a genuine mistake can be made, otherwise it is a question of how far away the police officers were when they observed the offence.

Chapter 7

A letter in mitigation

It is not every motoring offence that can be successfully defended. If you accept that the allegation is true or that your chances of success in fighting the case are negligible or worse, you will probably decide to plead Guilty. It is then a question of putting before the Court a favourable account of your driving in the hope of obtaining leniency. Fortunately, the majority of motoring summonses can be dealt with by post. Providing you exercise some care and accept that you must afford the Court a degree of respect, it is better to say something than nothing at all and this section of this book is devoted to assisting you compose a suitable letter in mitigation.

If you choose to write a letter you must be careful about what you say. A common mistake is to plead Guilty for reasons of convenience, but then set out chapter and verse which amount to saying that you are not really guilty of the offence at all. When a Court receives such a letter, it has to reject the guilty plea and substitute a plea of not guilty in its place. It will then arrange for the matter to be postponed so that witnesses can be called. When the motorist ultimately appears before the Court, if he then confirms his Guilty plea he may well be required to pay the prosecution costs and witness expenses. It is therefore essential to leave the Court in no doubt that you accept that you were at fault but nevertheless ask that they take certain circumstances into account in assessing the penalty.

The nature of the summons is explained on page 75. If it is a case where you are permitted to plead Guilty by post, then the summons and accompanying papers will tell you how to go about it. If the offence carries penalty points then you are required to send your driving licence to the Court. If it is at the Driver and Vehicle Licensing Centre for some reason, eg because you have changed your address, you should write to the Court explaining this and asking for an adjournment. If you have lost your licence you should tell the Court, and the police will then obtain a print-out from the DVLC, but you should still arrange to obtain a replacement licence yourself.

In cases where a Guilty plea may be entered by post, the summons will contain a "statement of facts" giving details of the alleged offence. If you do then plead Guilty by post, only that statement will be read out to the Court. However, it may happen that the statement does not entirely agree with your recollection of events and that even though you intend to plead Guilty you would like to set the record straight. You are entitled to dispute the statement of facts in any letter you write but you must be very careful to avoid giving the court the impression that you dispute your Guilt, or the Court will be faced with a conflict – that you have pleaded Guilty but your letter amounts to saying you are not Guilty. You could say something like "While I have read the Statement of facts I do not agree with .... because ...., but I nevertheless accept that I am Guilty of the offence." Whether you write a separate letter or complete the form which accompanies the summons is a matter of your choice.

Not every summons will give you the opportunity to plead Guilty by post. Unless the summons contains instructions giving you that facility you must attend Court yourself. You will usually be required to attend if the offence is fairly serious. You will be obliged to attend if disqualification is compulsory upon conviction for the particular offence – eg in a drink/driving case.

Even after writing a letter in mitigation it is possible

that a Court would require you to attend before them, because they are contemplating whether or not to disqualify you. This may arise in offences of driving without insurance, if there is a suggestion that it was done deliberately. It may also arise in instances of speeding when the speed has been calculated at more than 30 m.p.h. above the legal limit. If there is a hint of disqualification it would be wise to seek professional representation.

If you have been given a fixed penalty notice (see Chapter 5) it is clearly pointless writing a letter since the amount of the penalty is fixed.

Set out below are a variety of examples of letters that may be written. Before each letter there is a brief description of the circumstances. The letters are intended as a guide only and should be suitably amended to account for the circumstances in which you are involved. Where the offence is endorsable do not forget to send your driving licence with your letter. For those offences which carry a variable number of penalty points part of the suggested letters deal with that aspect. All letters should be addressed to the Clerk to the Justices of the relevant Magistrates' Court and should specify the day you are due before them, so that the Court can track down the correct papers and ensure your letter gets to the right Court at the right time.

While none of the letters which follow plead lack of funds as such, the amount of the fine and the manner in which it is to be paid may concern you. So far as the amount is concerned, you should have received a 'means enquiry' form of the kind described on page 83 with the summons that was sent to you. On the basis of the information you provide, the Court will assess the value of the units it imposes upon you (please see page 15 for a description of the unit fine system). If you do not provide the court with the necessary information, it can set whatever unit value it thinks fit given the little it knows about you (like where you live and what sort of car you were driving) and may, for example, decide to apply the maximum value of £100 per unit. In that event a typical speeding fine of 3 to 6 units could prove very expensive indeed (£300 to £600). Although the fine can be reduced if the unit value later proves to be inaccurate, this would necessitate a subsequent court appearance and that would detract more than somewhat from the convenience of pleading Guilty by post.

So far as the manner of payment is concerned, it is worth remembering that a fine is intended as a punishment and the Court will expect you to pay it in priority to other commitments. But in genuine cases you will be allowed time to pay. If you think you could pay the fine within 14 or 28 days then you should ask for that time. If you can only manage weekly instalments you should make an offer – it should be a sensible offer or the Court will not accept it and will fix a sum of their own.

No 1 No Driving Licence

Circumstances
A father borrows his son's 250 c.c. motor cycle to go down to the garage to buy replacement parts for his car which he is in the process of repairing before taking it for an MOT. He has never passed a motor cycle test but has driven cars for many years without incident. He is stopped by a police officer.

Letter:

Dear Sir

Police v A Motorist – Hearing 22nd October 1993 @ 2 p.m.

I acknowledge receipt of the summons and wish to plead Guilty to driving a motor cycle without the appropriate driving licence. I enclose my driving licence which permits me to drive motor cars and mopeds.

On the day in question I was repairing my car before taking it for an MOT. I realised I needed some spare parts. It was late on Saturday afternoon and the garage would close very shortly, so that I did not have time to take public transport. I therefore borrowed my son's 250 c.c. motor cycle and I was stopped by a police officer on my way back.

Unfortunately I did not realise at the time that I am not permitted to drive a motor cycle over 125 c.c. without having passed the motor cycle test. I genuinely thought I was covered under my own driving licence. I now realise my mistake and would like to apologise to the court. I would also like to reassure the Court that I will not commit this sort of offence again.

I have been driving for 20 years and I have never previously been prosecuted for any road traffic offence. I appreciate that I will receive a fine for this offence but I would be grateful if the Court could be as lenient as possible. I would be obliged if I could be permitted 28 days to pay the fine.

Yours faithfully

A Motorist

No 2 No Insurance

Circumstances

As a result of an accident, for which he was not responsible, a motorist is asked to produce his driving documents at the police station. He discovers that his insurance ran out three weeks previously. He had changed his address 6 months before but had forgotten to tell his insurance brokers.

Letter:

Dear Sir

Police v A Motorist – Hearing 22nd October 1993 @ 2 p.m.

I acknowledge receipt of the summons and I wish to plead Guilty to the offence of driving without insurance. I enclose my driving licence.

On Saturday 22nd June 1993 I was driving my motor car along Stoney Lane when another car came out of a side road and collided with me. I asked the police to attend and I believe that the other motorist is being prosecut ed for careless driving. I was then asked to produce my driving documents at the police station, which I did the following day. Unfortunately I discovered that my insur- ance had expired three weeks previously. This came as a great surprise as I thought it was due for renewal at the end of June, but in fact it had expired at the end of May. Unfortunately, I moved home at the beginning of the year and although I thought I had informed my insur- ance broker it appears they have no record of my new address. Apparently they sent my renewal notice to my previous address and it was not forwarded on to me. I hope that the Magistrates will accept that this was a genuine mistake on my part, and I would like to reassure them that I would never deliberately drive without insurance.

I appreciate that penalty points will be endorsed upon my driving licence. I hope that the Court will accept my explanation and in the circumstances impose only 6 penalty points. I also appreciate that I will be fined for the offence, and I would be grateful if the Court would permit me 28 days in which to pay this fine.

Yours faithfully

A Motorist

No 3 No MOT Certificate

Circumstances

On a spot check a motorist is asked to produce his dri- ving documents to the police station, but he realises his MOT certificate expired two weeks previously. He informs the police officer and is now prosecuted.

Letter:

Dear Sir

Police v A Motorist - Hearing 22nd October 1993 @ 2 p.m.

I acknowledge receipt of the summons and I wish to plead
guilty to using a motor vehicle without a current MOT
certificate.

On the day in question I was using my car when I was
stopped by a police officer on a spot check. I was asked
to produce my driving documents at the police station,
which I did. Unfortunately I discovered that my MOT certificate had run out two weeks previously. I did not
realise that it had expired, and the following day I
booked my car in for a test, which it passed without
difficulty. I apologise to the Court for having committed this offence but it was a genuine oversight on my
part. I would be grateful if I could be permitted 14
days to pay my fine.

Yours faithfully

A Motorist

No 4 No Tax Disc

Circumstances

A motorist pops down to the shops to buy some groceries,
not having realised that the tax disc had expired 21 days
previously. The vehicle is seen by a police officer and the
motorist is now prosecuted.

Letter:

Dear Sir

Police v A Motorist - Hearing 22nd October 1993 @ 2 p.m.

I acknowledge receipt of the summons and I would like to

plead Guilty to using my car without a current excise
licence. Unfortunately I did not notice that my tax disc
had expired and the very next day I bought a tax disc
which is now in my car. A few days before the offence
was committed I had returned from two weeks holiday. I
hope that the Magistrates will accept that this was a
genuine mistake on my part which I have now corrected. I
appreciate that I will be asked to pay a fine and I
would be grateful if the Court could kindly allow me 28
days in which to do so.

Yours faithfully

A Motorist

No 5 Defective Motor Vehicle

Circumstances

A young man driving a relatively ancient car is stopped by
police officers, who find he has two defective tyres and
there is excess travel in his brake pedal. He therefore
receives three summonses, two for the tyres and one for
the brakes.

Letter:

Dear Sir

Police v A Motorist - Hearing 22nd October 1993 @ 2 p.m.

I acknowledge receipt of the three summonses and I would
like to plead Guilty to each of them. I enclose my driving licence upon which there is only one endorsement
which was for speeding some 12 months ago.

On the day in question I was driving back from college
and I was stopped by police officers, who told me that I
had defective tyres and that there was excess travel in
my footbrake. I had purchased the vehicle from a friend
three months before and I had only used it to go to and
from college. I did not realise that there was insuffi-
cient tread on the two tyres. I do inspect my vehicle

regularly, but tread was worn on the inside of the tyres and therefore not easy to see. I accept that there was some travel in the footbrake, but it was nonetheless quite capable of bringing my vehicle to a stop. I have now been able to correct the brakes and have since purchased two tyres. The vehicle has just recently passed its MOT.

I would like to apologise for these offences and to reassure the Court that they will not occur again. Unfortunately as a student I am only in receipt of a grant and in the circumstances I should be grateful if the Court would kindly allow me to discharge the fine at a rate of £5 per week.

Yours faithfully

A. Motorist

No 6 Speeding

Circumstances

A motorist travelling along a dual carriageway that is subject to a 40 m.p.h. speed limit is observed to be travelling at 55 m.p.h.

Letter:

Dear Sir:

Police v A Motorist – Hearing 22nd October 1993 @ 2 p.m.

I acknowledge receipt of the summons which alleges that I exceeded the speed limit and I would like to plead guilty. I enclose my driving licence.

I agree that on the day in question I was travelling along Stratford Road at a speed of 55 m.p.h. I accept that the speed limit on this dual carriageway is 40 m.p.h. I realise that I should not have been travelling as fast as I was. It is a very good road with clear visibility and unfortunately since there were virtually no vehicles on the road I allowed myself to go faster than

I ought to have done. I would like to apologise for what
I have done and I would like to reassure the court that
I will be very much more careful and obey speed limits
in the future.

   I appreciate that my driving licence will be endorsed
and that I will be required to pay a fine. I would
respectfully suggest that 3 penalty points would be
appropriate and I should be grateful if the court would
kindly allow me 28 days in order to pay the fine.

Yours faithfully

A. Motorist

No 7 Careless Driving

Circumstances

A motorist drives along a minor road and comes to a
junction. He wishes to turn right. As he looks both ways
and it appears to be clear he proceeds forward. He is suddenly involved in a collision with a motor cyclist who
strikes the offside of his car.

Letter:

Dear Sir

Police v A Motorist - Hearing 22nd October 1993 @ 2 p.m.

I acknowledge receipt of the summons which alleges that
I drove without due care and attention. I wish to enter
a plea of guilty and I enclose my driving licence.

   I accept that on the day in question I was driving my
car along the Cranmore Boulevard towards the junction
with Stratford Road. It was my intention to turn right.
I waited at the junction to allow vehicles to pass along
the main road. I then looked both ways and it appeared
to be clear. I began to move forward when suddenly I was
struck by a motor cyclist who collided with the offside
of my car. I have thought very carefully about the circumstances of the accident and realise that although I

had looked to my right I must have missed seeing the approaching motor cyclist. It may be that my vision was obstructed by overhanging trees or parked vehicles that were on the right hand side of the road. When I pulled forward I genuinely believed that it was clear and safe to proceed. When the motor cyclist came into my vision I braked but unfortunately a collision occurred. I believe that he may have been travelling faster than the speed limit, but I accept that it is my obligation to ensure that it is safe before pulling out.

I have been driving for 15 years and I have never previously been prosecuted for any sort of motoring offence. I hope that the Magistrates will accept that this was a moment of misjudgement on my part and that I am normally a very careful driver.

I appreciate that my driving licence will be endorsed with penalty points. I believe that in the circumstances 3 penalty points would be appropriate. I also appreciate that I will be required to pay a fine and I would be grateful if the Court would accept my offer of £10 a week.

Yours faithfully

A Motorist

No 8 Careless Driving

Circumstances

A motorist wishes to turn right at a set of traffic lights. His vision is obstructed, to some extent, by vehicles which have been travelling in the opposite direction also wishing to turn right. He cannot complete his turn immediately because of oncoming vehicles but when he believes there is a suitable gap he turns and is struck by a car coming in the opposite direction.

Letter:

Dear Sir

<u>Police v A Motorist - Hearing 22nd October 1993 @ 2 p.m.</u>

I acknowledge receipt of the summons and wish to plead
guilty to the allegation of driving without due care and
attention. I enclose my driving licence. On the 15th
July I wished to turn right at the traffic light controlled junction of School Road and Stratford Road. When
I first approached the junction the lights were red and
when they changed to green I moved forward. There were
vehicles coming in the opposite direction also intending
to turn right and, to some extent, this obscured my
vision of oncoming vehicles wishing to go straight on. I
waited where I was for some time until I believed that a
suitable gap had appeared in oncoming traffic. Before I
turned right I looked to see if it was clear to do so,
and in the honest and genuine belief that it was, I commenced my manoeuvre. When I had almost completed my turn
I was struck by an oncoming vehicle in the rear nearside
of my car.

I accept that it is my obligation when turning right
to do so only when I have made certain it is clear and
safe to proceed. I trust that the Court will accept that
I was taking steps to carry out this manoeuvre safely
and I did look. I do not know where the other vehicle
came from and can only presume that it was obscured from
my vision by a large van wishing to turn right. Since I
almost completed my manoeuvre before the collision
occurred, I believe that the other motorist may have
been travelling rather faster than would have been
appropriate for the road conditions or otherwise might
have had ample opportunity in which to slow down and
stop without a collision occurring. However, I accept
that the standard of my driving on this occasion fell
below that expected by the Court and I apologise for the
incident.

I appreciate that, as a consequence of conviction,
penalty points will be endorsed on my driving licence. I
understand that the range of points is between 3 and 9
but, given the circumstances of this particular inci-

dent, I would respectfully suggest to the Court that 3
or 4 penalty points would be appropriate. Due to heavy
financial commitments, the best offer I can make is
£10.00 per week and I trust that the Court will find
this satisfactory.

Yours faithfully

A Motorist

No 9 Careless Driving

Circumstances

On a wet and miserable day in February, a motorist is
driving along a trunk road and encounters a left hand
bend. The speed limit for the road in question is 60 miles
per hour and he is travelling at 50 miles per hour. He is,
unfortunately, driving too quickly for the road conditions
and skids on the bend with the consequence that he goes
onto the wrong side of the road and collides with a vehicle
coming in the opposite direction.

Letter:

Dear Sir

Police v A Motorist – Hearing 22nd October 1993 @ 2 p.m.

I acknowledge receipt of the summons alleging that I
drove without due care and attention on 13 February 1993
and I would like to plead guilty. I enclose my driving
licence, which has one previous endorsement for careless
driving.

On 13th February 1993 I was driving my motor car along
the A456 on my way home. The road in question is subject
to a 60 mile per hour speed limit and I was travelling
at approximately 50 miles per hour. The weather was very
poor. It was raining heavily and the road surface was
wet. I believed that I was driving at a speed which was
safe, given the road conditions but unfortunately, as I

entered a left hand bend my car skidded and as a consequence I collided with a vehicle coming in the opposite direction.

At the material time I was complying with the speed limit. Indeed, I was travelling about 10 miles per hour below that. Unfortunately however I now accept that I had been travelling too quickly for the prevailing road conditions. I had not anticipated that the road surface would be as slippery as it was and, unfortunately, whilst travelling around the bend the rear end of my car began to skid and as a consequence, despite my efforts to control my vehicle, I crossed onto the wrong side of the road and collided with a vehicle coming in the opposite direction.

I appreciate that as a consequence of conviction penalty points will be endorsed on my driving licence. I trust that the Court will accept that this was a minor error of judgement on my part and that I was taking a certain amount of care. I would respectfully suggest that 3 or 4 penalty points would be appropriate. I further appreciate that, as a consequence of conviction, I will be required to pay a fine. I would be grateful if I could be allowed 28 days in order to pay.

Yours faithfully

A Motorist

No 10 Careless Driving

Circumstances

In the course of driving home in the rush hour traffic a motorist collides with the rear of the vehicle directly in front of him. That vehicle slowed down quickly and at the last moment indicated to turn left. The motorist did not anticipate the manoeuvre but clearly he was too close to avoid an accident.

Letter:

Dear Sir

Police v A Motorist - Hearing 22nd October 1993 @ 2 p.m.

I acknowledge receipt of the summons alleging that I drove without due care and attention. I wish to enter a plea of guilty and I enclose my driving licence.

I agree that at the time in question I was driving along Quinton Road in the direction of Harborne when I became involved in a collision with another vehicle which was directly in front of me. I was driving home in the rush hour traffic. Motor vehicles had been moving at approximately 25 m.p.h. There was no apparent indication of slowing down. Suddenly and without any adequate warning the vehicle in front of me slowed down considerably and at the last moment indicated to turn left at a road junction. I had not anticipated that manoeuvre and I braked heavily, but unfortunately I was unable to avoid a collision due to the damp road surface.

I believe that the other motorist must take a major part of the responsibility for the accident. If he had exercised caution, then he would have given a signal well before the junction. This would have allowed me to slow down in the usual way. Instead he braked sharply and indicated left at the same time. I trust that the Magistrates will accept that, in rush hour traffic, it is often difficult to keep a distance behind the vehicle in front, which would enable a driver to come to a stop in the event of something unusual happening. Although I consider the other motorist was largely at fault, I accept that my obligation is to remain a sufficient distance behind him, in order to stop in such circumstances. I agree that I failed to drive with all due care and attention but nevertheless believe I exercised a substantial amount of care.

I appreciate that in respect of this offence penalty points will be endorsed on my driving licence. In the circumstances I respectfully believe that 3 penalty points would be appropriate. I appreciate that I will also be required to pay a fine and I hope that the magistrates will be as lenient as possible. I would also be grateful if I could be permitted 28 days in order to pay the fine.

Yours faithfully

A Motorist

No 11 Failure to Comply with a Traffic Sign

Circumstances
A motorist is approaching a set of traffic lights which are green and then change to amber. He believes that he can get across the lights before they change to red, but unfortunately he does not make it. He is observed by police officers who subsequently stop him.

Letter:

Dear Sir

<u>Police v A Motorist – Hearing 22nd October 1993 @ 2 p.m</u>.

I acknowledge receipt of the summons alleging that I failed to comply with a set of traffic lights. I wish to enter a plea of guilty and I enclose my driving licence.

I accept that on the day in question I was driving along Shaftsmoor Lane approaching the junction with Stratford Road, which is controlled by traffic lights. On my approach to the lights they were green, but as I got close they changed to amber. I was only a short distance from the lights and I believed that if I braked I might cause a vehicle behind me to collide with my vehicle. I therefore decided to proceed, believing this to be the safest course. Unfortunately it would appear that when I was only a matter of two or three feet from the stop line the lights changed to red. At that stage I believed there was nothing I could do, so I proceeded. I accept therefore that I crossed those lights while they were red but I would like to reassure the Court that there was no prospect of an accident occurring.

I appreciate that I will receive penalty points for

this offence and that I will be required to pay a fine.
I would be grateful if the court would be as lenient as
possible towards me and allow me 28 days in which to pay
the fine.

Yours faithfully

A Motorist

No 12 Pedestrian Crossing

Circumstances

A motorist who is driving along a road approaches a zebra
crossing. The road is quite wide and there is no central
reservation in the crossing. When he gets near the crossing itself the pedestrian on the other side of the road
begins to walk across. The motorist decides to proceed.
He is stopped by a police officer on foot patrol a few yards
further down the road.

Letter:

Dear Sir

<u>Police v A Motorist – Hearing 22nd October 1993 @ 2 p.m.</u>

I acknowledge receipt of the summons alleging that I
failed to give way to a pedestrian on the pedestrian
crossing. I would like to enter a plea of guilty and I
enclose my driving licence.

I accept that on the day in question I was driving
along Stratford Road approaching a zebra crossing. I was
travelling at approximately 25 m.p.h. and when I was
some distance from the crossing I looked to see if there
were any pedestrians likely to use it. I did not see any
and therefore I decided to proceed. When I was only a
short distance from the crossing I observed a man begin
to cross from the other side of the road. At that stage
it would not have been possible for me to come to a stop
so I continued on. When I drove across the crossing the

pedestrian was some considerable distance away.

The only reason I am pleading guilty is because I realise this to be an absolute offence. I appreciate that if a pedestrian puts his foot on the black and white markings before my vehicle reaches them, I am obliged to stop. However, there was never any prospect of a collision, and indeed if I had attempted to come to a stop it is likely the vehicle travelling behind me would have collided with my car. I appreciate that penalty points will be endorsed on my driving licence and I will be required to pay a fine. I would be grateful if the Court would be as lenient as possible toward me and allow me 28 days to pay the fine.

Yours faithfully

A Motorist

No 13 Failure to Produce Documents

Circumstances

A motorist is asked to produce his driving documents following a spot check. He is able to locate his driving licence and his certificate of insurance but he cannot find his MOT. His obligation is to produce all documents within 7 days. He produces what he can and is prosecuted for failing to provide an MOT certificate.

Letter:

Dear Sir

Police v A Motorist – Hearing 22nd October 1993 @ 2 p.m.

I acknowledge receipt of the summons alleging that I failed to produce my MOT certificate and I wish to plead Guilty.

While I was on my way home I was stopped by a police officer and asked to produce my driving documents to a police station within 7 days. On arrival at home I sort-ed out my driving licence and certificate of insurance, but unfortunately I was unable to locate my MOT certificate. Despite a search through my papers at home I was unable to find the document. I attended the police station and explained the circumstances. About two weeks later I came across the document and although I went to the police station with it, I was told I was to be prosecuted. I trust that the Magistrates will accept that I did make every effort to find the document in question, but was unable to do so. I appreciate that I am likely to be liable to a fine but would ask the court to be as lenient as possible and permit me 14 days to pay it.

Yours faithfully

A Motorist

No 14 Failure to Comply with a Road Sign

Circumstances

In the course of a long journey a motorist decides to overtake a line of slower moving vehicles but in the process of doing so, encounters a solid line on his side of the road. He cannot get back in time and is seen by a police officer to travel 20 yards on the wrong side of that line.

Letter:

Dear Sir

Police v A Motorist - Hearing 22nd October 1993 @ 2 p.m.

I acknowledge receipt of the summons alleging that I failed to comply with double white lines on 31 May 1993. I wish to plead Guilty and enclose my driving licence.

While travelling along the A5 I encountered 3 slow moving lorries. I remained behind them until it was safe to overtake. As I was in the process of passing the third vehicle I became aware that I was approaching a solid white line on my side of the road. When I commenced my manoeuvre I could not see any warning signs indicating that I was approaching a restricted area. There were no vehicles coming in the opposite direction at any time during the course of overtaking. I overtook the vehicles in complete safety but, unfortunately, I was not able to return to my side of the road until after I had passed the commencement of the solid white line. I did, however, return to the nearside within a few yards of doing so.

I would like to emphasise to the Court that these were not two solid white lines but one solid white line on my side of the road. At no time was there any prospect of an accident because visibility of approaching vehicles was good. I appreciate that I have committed an offence of crossing a solid white line, but, having committed myself to the overtaking manoeuvre it was clearly safer to proceed, rather than try to squeeze myself back in between the second and third vehicles.

I hope that the Court will take these circumstances into account in assessing the financial penalty. I would be obliged if the Court would kindly allow me 28 days in order to pay the fine.

Yours faithfully

A Motorist

No 15 Dangerous Parking

Circumstances

A motorist parks his car on a modest incline in order to go into a paper shop. While in the shop he hears a bang and upon going outside discovers that his car has rolled backwards down the slope and into collision with a parked car. When the police arrive the brakes are checked and found to be in order.

Letter:

Dear Sir

<u>Police v A Motorist – Hearing 22nd October 1993 @ 2 p.m</u>.

I acknowledge receipt of the summons alleging that I parked my vehicle in a dangerous position and I wish to plead Guilty. I enclose my driving licence. It is my usual practice to buy a morning newspaper from my local newsagent on my way to work. On the 16th April, I parked my car outside the newsagent, which is situated in West Street. This is on an incline and I applied my hand-brake, got out of my car and went into the shop. As I was about to buy my paper, I heard a collision outside and went out to investigate. To my horror, I saw that my vehicle had rolled backwards down the hill and collided with the front of a parked car which was situated behind my vehicle. I could not understand how this had occurred, since I believed that I had securely parked my car by putting on the handbrake. The police arrived sub-sequently and tested my brakes. They were found to be in working order. I can only assume that I must have failed to put the handbrake on completely. I did apply the handbrake to some extent, because otherwise my vehicle would have started to roll backwards as soon as I stopped. I had time to get out of my car and go into the paper shop before the collision occurred.

I hope the Court will accept that on this occasion I made a minor misjudgement. Unfortunately this incident has already cost me a considerable sum because my car was only insured for third party risks. I have had to pay for the cost of repairs to my own vehicle out of my own pocket. In the circumstances I trust that the Court will be as lenient as possible towards me. I would be obliged if the Court would allow me 14 days to pay the fine.

Yours faithfully

A Motorist

No 16 Motorway Offences

Circumstances

A motorist, who is towing a trailer behind his car, is observed by a police officer to move into the third lane and his speed is checked at 75 miles per hour. He is now prosecuted for speeding and for an offence against the Motorway Regulations.

Letter:

Dear Sir

<u>Police v A Motorist - Hearing 22nd October 1993 @ 2 p.m.</u>

I acknowledge receipt of the summons alleging that I exceeded the speed limit and drove my vehicle while towing a trailer in the third lane of the motorway. I wish to plead guilty to both offences and enclose my driving licence.

I accept that on 14 June 1993 I was travelling southbound on the M1 motorway at a speed of approximately 60 miles per hour. I then encountered a slow moving lorry which was occupying the centre lane. I remained behind this vehicle quite some distance but there appeared to be no prospect of its returning to the nearside lane. While driving behind the lorry my speed was reduced to approximately 50 miles per hour. I then decided to overtake the lorry but, before doing so, ensured that there were no vehicles using the overtaking lane and I indicated my intention to overtake. I accelerated and returned to the middle as soon as I had completed the manoeuvre.

I accept that by accelerating I increased my speed to over 60 miles per hour but I am far from certain that it was as much as 75 miles per hour. I now realise that I am not permitted to go more than 60 miles per hour when towing a trailer. This was the first time I had ever towed a trailer on the motorway and I did not fully appreciate that I was prevented from using the overtaking lane. I would like to reassure the Court that there is no prospect of this sort of offence arising again and

I would like to apologise for my mistake.

I appreciate that I will be required to pay fines in respect of both offences, but I would ask the Court to be as lenient towards me as possible. Due to certain financial commitments which I have, the best offer I can make is to pay the fine at the rate of £10 per week and I trust that the court will find this satisfactory.

Yours faithfully

A Motorist

No 17 Lighting your Vehicle

Circumstances

A motorist is stopped by a police officer because his back light is defective in that it was broken and was showing some white light to the rear.

Letter:

Dear Sir

<u>Police v A Motorist – Hearing 22nd October 1993 @ 2 p.m</u>.

I acknowledge receipt of the summons alleging that I drove a vehicle with a defective back light on the 4th August 1993 and I wish to plead guilty to that offence.

Approximately two days before the offence occurred, a motorist ran into the back of my car causing some minor damage. Unfortunately, the rear nearside light cluster was damaged to some extent and part of the red glass was missing. I tried to buy a replacement part immediately, but it was not available and had to be specially ordered. I accept that I committed the offence on this occasion and that with hindsight I should have masked over the damaged area. I trust that the court will accept that I was taking positive steps in order to rectify the problem and I wish to reassure the Court that this sort of offence will not occur again. I should be grateful if the court would kindly permit me 28 days in order to pay the fine.

Yours faithfully

A Motorist

No 18 Seat Belts

Circumstances
A motorist is seen to be driving without a seat belt. He had bruised his chest a few days before the incident and found it uncomfortable to wear a seat belt.

Letter:

Dear Sir

<u>Police v A Motorist – Hearing 22nd October 1993 @ 2 p.m</u>.

I acknowledge receipt of the summons alleging that on the 8th July 1993 I drove my vehicle without wearing a seat belt. I wish to plead guilty to that offence.

I always ensure that I and my passengers wear seat belts on all occasions. Regrettably, a few days before this incident I had bruised my chest in a fall and, as a consequence, I found it uncomfortable to wear my seat belt. I appreciate that I am required by law to wear a seat belt at all times and this is my normal practice. I hope, however, that the court will take the circumstances into account when assessing the financial penalty and I would like to reassure the Court that I will always wear a seat belt in the future. I would be grateful if I could be permitted 14 days to pay the fine.

Yours faithfully

A Motorist

Appendix

Motoring penalties at a glance

The table which follows is intended to provide you with useful information about the penalties that are imposed by the Courts for the various motoring offences discussed in this book. The maximum financial penalties are listed, together with the number of penalty points. The unit fine likely to be imposed by the Court is also set out but, as mentioned in Chapter 1, it is important to remember that this is a guide only. It applies to an average offence of the kind in question coupled with a prompt Guilty plea and no aggravating factors like deliberately bad or excessively fast driving. Magistrates will take a variety of circumstances into account when imposing a unit fine upon a particular motorist – for example, higher fines are more likely when the circumstances of the offence are serious. Also shown are the fixed penalties which may be applied if you are not prosecuted.

Where a conviction takes place after a contested case, it is usual for you to be required to pay the prosecution's costs and witness expenses in addition to the fine. The extent of these further sums will vary from case to case.

The Court expects a fine to be discharged quickly, but if it cannot be paid immediately then time to pay will usually be granted. This is explained on page 95.

If the fine is not required to be paid immediately, the court will usually inform you in writing of how it is to be discharged and when and where it is to be paid. If there is a significant alteration in your financial circumstances, you may apply to the court for permission to pay the fine by lower instalments, but this will usually require your attendance at court and full details of your financial position.

If you fail or refuse to pay a fine, then a warrant for your arrest may be issued and if it is still not paid you could be sent to prison as an alternative punishment.

Description of offence	Maximum fine	The likely fine in units	Fixed penalty	Penalty points	Remarks	See page
1. a) Driving licences Driving without a licence or without the appropriate licence	£1,000	5	£40	3 – 6	Not endorsable in every case	18
b) "Provisional licence" offences (i) Driving a motor car whilst not accompanied by a qualified driver	£1,000	4	£40	3 – 6	Disqualification is sometimes considered	20
(ii) Motor cyclist carrying un-qualified passenger	£1,000	3	£40	3 – 6	Disqualification is sometimes considered	20
(iii) No "L" plates	£1,000	2	£40	3 – 6		20
2. Driving without insurance	£5,000	15	N/A	6 – 8	A very serious offence. If committed deliberately you could expect to be disqualified or at least receive 7 or 8 points. If committed inadvertently the fine and points would be less.	22

Description of offence	Maximum fine	The likely fine in units	Fixed penalty	Penalty points	Remarks	See page
3. MOT and tax disc						
a) No MOT	£1,000	3	£40	N/A		24
b) No tax disc						
(i) No disc in force	£1,000 or 5 times duty lost if greater	The duty lost + twice that amount or 4 units, whichever is greater	N/A		If there is a claim for back-duty and this has not been paid before you appear before the Court, it will be added to the fine	24
(ii) Failing to display a tax disc	£200	1	£20			
(iii) Fraudulent use of a tax disc	£5,000	10	N/A			
4. Roadworthy condition Defective brakes, steering or tyres or a vehicle in a dangerous condition	£2,500	4	£40	3		26
5. Speeding	£1,000	3 – 8 depending on the excess	£40	3 – 6	Disqualification will be considered if the speed limit is exceeded by 30 or more miles per hour.	29

6. *Pedestrian crossings –*
Traffic lights & road
signs

(i) Failing to give precedence	£1,000	3	£40	3	Disqualification sometimes imposed	32
(ii) Overtaking within the zig-zag lines	£1,000	3	£40	3	It is only an offence to overtake before the crossing	
(iii) Parking within the zig-zags	£1,000	3	£40	3		
(iv) Failing to comply with traffic lights	£1,000	3	£40	3	Amber means "stop" unless unsafe to do so. There is a 3 second gap between the green and red signals so you should have plenty of time in which to stop in safety	33
(v) Failing to comply with road signs	£1,000	3	£40 if endorsable; £20 if not	3 (not in all cases)		

Description of offence	Maximum fine	The likely fine in units	Fixed penalty	Penalty points	Remarks	See page
7. Careless driving	£2,500	6	N/A	3 – 9	The fine and points that will be imposed will depend upon the extent of the carelessness	34
8. Dangerous driving	£5,000 and/or 6 months in prison	20 – 30	N/A	3 – 11 (if not disqualified)	Do not try and deal with an allegation of this nature without legal advice. Disqualification for at least 12 months is almost certain, as is a retest	36
9. Failing to stop and report						37
a) Failing to stop after an accident	£5,000 and/or 6 months in prison	10	N/A	5 – 10		
b) Failing to report an accident	£5,000 and/or 6 months in prison	10	N/A	5 – 10	A period of disqualification is likely to be imposed where both offences have been committed	

Offence	Max fine					Page
10. *Failure to produce documents*	£1,000	2	N/A			40
11. *Dangerous parking and obstruction*						41
a) Dangerous parking	£1,000	3	£40	3		
b) Obstructing the highway	£1,000 (£2,500 in certain cases)	2	£20			
12. *Motorway offences*						42
a) Driving in reverse	£2,500	12	N/A	3	If offence committed on a main carriageway;	
		4	N/A	3	If offence committed on slip road	
b) Driving in wrong direction	£2,500	20	N/A	3	If on main carriageway;	
		6	N/A	3	If offence committed on slip road. Disqualification will be considered in both these cases	

Description of offence	Maximum fine	The likely fine in units	Fixed penalty	Penalty points	Remarks	See page
c) Driving off the carriageway	£2,000	6	N/A	3	If driven along central reservation;	42
		5	N/A	3	If driven along hard shoulder	
d) Making a "U" turn	£2,500	16	N/A	3	Disqualification will be considered	
e) Stopping on the hard shoulder	£2,500	4	N/A		If on a main motorway;	
		2	N/A		If on a slip road	
13. *Driving without lights*	£1,000	3	£20			43
14. *Drinking and driving offences* a) Driving or attempting to drive with excess alcohol or whilst unfit	£5,000	20 – 40 depending on alcohol level	N/A	(3 – 11) if not disqualified	Disqualification of at least 12 months will be imposed. See text for longer disqualification	63

b) Refusal to provide a specimen for analysis	£5,000	24	N/A	(3 – 11) if not disqualified	Disqualification for 18 months very likely	64
c) In charge of a motor vehicle with excess alcohol or whilst unfit or refusing to provide a specimen when in charge	£2,500	12	N/A	10	Disqualification a distinct possibility	63
d) Refusing a roadside breath test	£1,000	6	N/A	4		58
15. *Stolen vehicles*						
a) Taking a vehicle without owner's consent	£5,000 and/or 6 months in prison	12 – 15	N/A		A custodial sentence is a distinct possibility	46
b) Allowing yourself to be carried in a stolen motor vehicle	£5,000 and/or 6 months in prison	8 – 10	N/A			
16. *Seat belts*						
a) Not wearing	£500	2 2 (front)	£20			45
b) Child not wearing	£500	1 (rear)	£20			

Index

lighting of vehicle, 44-45, 90, 114-115
MOT, 25-26, 86, 97-98
motorway offences, 30, 43, 45, 90, 113-114
obstruction, 42-43, 89-90
parking, 42, 89-90, 111-112
pedestrian crossing, 32-33, 88, 108-109
road signs, 34-35, 88, 110-111
seat belt, 46-47, 91, 115
seriousness of, 16
speeding, 29-32, 87, 100-101
tax disc, 26, 86, 98-99
theft of a vehicle, 47-48
traffic lights, 33-34, 88, 107-108
vehicle theft, 47-48

Parking, 42, 89-90, 111-112
Pedestrian crossing, 32-33, 88, 108-109
Pelican crossing, 32-33
Penalty points, 12, 15, 49-56, 71-73
Photographic evidence, 18-19, 73-74
Police, reporting accident to, 12-13, 38-41
Prosecution:
    avoiding, 14
    warning of, 13-14
Provisional licence, 19, 20
Punishment – see *Disqualification, Fines, Penalty points*

Radar speed gun, 30-31
Reasonable consideration, driving without, 35-36, 88-89,
    101-107
Retesting, 38
Road fund licence, 26, 86, 98-99
Road signs, 34-35, 88, 110-111
Roof rack, 29

Seat belt, 46-47, 91, 115
Seriousness of offence, 16
Solicitor, when needed, 15, 37, 77-78
Specimen, failing to provide, 64
Speeding, 29-32, 87, 100-101
Statements, 12, 79-81
Steering, 27, 86-87
Stop, failure to after an accident, 38-39